a quarter-to-seven. Hardly worth going to sleep. He'll be woken up again at half-seven. Then he's got to catch up on all the work he's missed at college. He's really falling behind. Still, worry about that later . . . for now, he'll just think about Becky.

But he's barely closed his eyes when his door bangs open and he hears his father calling his name. Adam keeps his eyes shut. Just pretend to be asleep, but his heart's thumping insanely. What can have happened?

Now his father's calling his name again and then he pulls all the covers off his bed. Adam squints round. He can hardly speak.

'Dad,' he gasps, 'what's happened?'

'You can stop pretending,' snarls his father. 'And I want you downstairs, NOW.'

to see Pete Johnson's books. Here are their comments on *Discovery*.

'My favourite bit was Jason's dream. It was excellent and really weird, especially the bit about the funeral and Adam's girlfriend. I like the way you told us it had happened before.'

'Jason's changed a lot in the book. He seems to have realised that he can let the cool mask slip once in a while and open up to people like Cathy. You let out many secrets of Jason's mysterious character and that added a lot of feeling and emotion. You found yourself imagining what he must have been going through, especially as everyone looks up to him.'

'Adam and Becky make a strong couple. The scene at the synagogue was brilliant. I really felt for Becky.'

'Mark and Cathy are my favourite characters. Mark makes me laugh and I know so many people like him. Cathy seems to be changing a lot. The ending was brilliant but a real shock. I am glad Cathy is getting some romance at last.'

'I think Jason feels something for Cathy. Am I right? I reckon he's scared to tell Cathy. Reading the book makes me wish I could help Jason.'

FRIENDS FOREVER ③

PETE JOHNSON DISCOVERY

ST. BRENDAN'S HIGH SCHOOL

Laura   Jez   Becky   Azam   Jason   Mark

mammoth

First published in Great Britain 1992
by Mammoth
Reissued 1998 by Mammoth
an imprint of Reed International Books Limited
Michelin House, 81 Fulham Road, London SW3 6RB

ISBN 0 7497 0649 X

1 3 5 7 9 10 8 6 4 2

A CIP catalogue record for this title
is available from the British Library

Printed and bound in Great Britain
by Cox & Wyman Ltd, Reading, Berkshire

Contents

Also by Pete Johnson

The Cool Boffin
The Dead Hour
I'd Rather Be Famous
One Step Beyond
Secrets from the School Underground
The Vision
We, the Haunted

the 'Friends Forever' series

No Limits
Break Out
Discovery
Everything Changes

for younger readers

Secret Friend

With love and special thanks to Liza, Jan, Melissa Vardy, Margherita Valenti, Bill Bloomfield.

Yo!

Mark here, writing to you about *Friends Forever I* and *Friends Forever II*. I've got to remind you of all the good bits.

The book stars Jason, Cathy, Adam, Jez, Lauren and moi. We all live in the same (boring) village and also all went to school in the town. This meant most of the kids in the village hated us. One night, one lucky person (guess who) got caught up by a gang of local kids and got beaten up. After that, we never went anywhere alone. And we even had our secret hiding place, a hut no one knew about.

Anyway, steaming on now. When we were about fifteen the hassle from the village kids stopped but the six of us were still, what's the word, a group. No more than that. Anyway, (I must stop using that word. I'll ban it from the rest of the letter) we looked out for each other. Then, Lauren and Jason started going out – until Jason turned up at Lauren's fifteenth birthday party with another girl on his arm. NIGHTMARE.

They didn't speak for a year after that. But then, Lauren started getting these unsigned notes saying, "Sorry." You can guess who they're from. In my opinion, they're just desperate to go out together again, and I know about these things.

But meanwhile, Lauren has been seeing our English teacher, Grant. She's only gone out with him a couple of times (three, I think, not sure) but she's had grief from everyone over that. Especially the people in our English group. You see, Lauren's started getting grade As and everyone thinks, well, you know.

And my mate, Adam, is going out with a really, really beautiful, wonderful girl, called Becky (yeah, I fancy her too). His parents are strict Jews and believe he can only get serious with another Jewish girl. So Adam and Becky have been meeting secretly at night in our old hut. Only, at Adam's party, his mum caught Adam and Becky having a quick cuddle.

I'm running out of paper. Quick. What else? Cathy organised a demonstration against eating meat, outside Radley's, which was a big success (Jason and I also helped). Cathy's mum is going out with this bloke, Giles, who Cathy hates. Now, Giles has moved into Cathy's house, which she's none too pleased about. And – oh yeah – I sang at a Karaoke and, if I say so myself, was a bit of a hit.

But the really big news is that Lauren is going to Swanks with Grant tonight, where she is going to tell him she doesn't want to see him any more. She's not looking forward to this, well, it's quite hard finishing with your tutor, isn't it? But what she doesn't know is that Jason is also going to Swanks, where he's hoping to whisk her off on his white charger. Well, Adam's motorbike, actually, which Jason's borrowing for the night.

Will Lauren get the courage to finish with Grant? What's Jason going to do at Swanks? Are Jason and Lauren finally going to get together . . . and when do I get a girlfriend?

😟 That's a picture of me wondering.

I'll let you go and see Jason now. Besides, I've run out of paper and you'll get the cardboard back of this pad if I don't stop now.

See you a bit later, then.

Good times.

Mark

The Black Knight to the Rescue

Adam and Jason solemnly shake hands. Normally, it would sound corny to say, 'Good Luck' but Adam risks it and it doesn't. Not tonight.

'You look just like the dungeon master,' says Adam. For Jason's dressed entirely in black; black polo-neck, black leather jacket, black jeans. For the first time that evening, Jason grins. Then he slides on to Adam's motorbike. He sits there, not saying anything. Adam wonders if he's psyching himself up. Funny, you never think of Jason needing to do that. At last, he revs the engine, mutters, 'Cheers for the loan, mate,' and then he's gone.

It's only about eleven o'clock but already there's that deathly quiet you get in musty old villages. A few lights are visible behind thick curtains but most houses are already dark and as still as a corpse. A dog with an annoying high-pitched bark, the rumble of traffic and the occasional train, is the only proof that life still beats on. Yet, this is the kind of night Jason

1

likes best. No human beings, no moon, no stars, nothing to stop the darkness wrapping itself around you.

Tonight, the darkness is all powerful and Jason's a part of that darkness. The Black Knight, roaring to rescue a girl. *The* girl. His destination – Swanks nightclub. Only, he's going in totally the wrong direction. Now, he's riding down a deserted alley, where giant banks of weeds sway and hiss and a cat suddenly stirs in the middle of them, its eyes huge and staring. This is a short-cut to a place where the houses sprawl contentedly and, even in the dark, all the lawns gleam as if they've just been polished.

And there it is, Lauren's house. How often, late at night, after riding for hours on his bicycle (in the day, Jason considers anyone over ten who rides a bike rather dodgy but at night, no rules apply), did he end up here. How often had he climbed over the gate and stood on the gravel, staring up at her bedroom window. It used to send him crazy; there she was, just a few feet away from him and yet, just as far from him as she could be, in that strangest and most private of countries, behind her eyelids. Then he'd have this mad urge to wake her up. A couple of times he even had the stones in his hand, all ready to smash his way into her dreams.

But tonight, he has no stones to throw. He doesn't even climb over her gate. What's the point? She isn't there. She's at Swanks, with that slime, Grant . . . where Jason should be. So why isn't he? Because, all the time this killer thought is drumming away in his head. What if Lauren doesn't want to be rescued from Grant? She could be perfectly happy going out with her tutor; he's educated, got money, a car, can take her to expensive restaurants. How can Jason be sure she needs help? The answer is, he can't. It's just a feeling. But, HE MIGHT BE WRONG.

He could be riding into the most humiliating night of his life. A nightmare from which he will never awaken: rejection. He hardly dares say the word. So what is he to do? Risk it. She's worth it, isn't she? Yes, definitely. Well, go on then. But he doesn't move, perhaps he can't. He just stands, staring up at Lauren's house, like a lone sentry, lost in thought.

A woman Lauren's never seen before jabs a well-manicured hand on to her shoulder. The woman gives Lauren a small, tight smile. 'You're looking lost,' she says. 'It is rather overwhelming, isn't it?' How patronising this woman sounds. Lauren immediately bristles. Actually, she'd been standing, for what seemed like several days, listening to Grant having this incredibly boring conversation with a couple whose names she'd instantly forgotten, until she could bear it no longer. So she'd edged away, only to be faced by this woman, with a huge face, jet black hair and far too much powder on her face, which makes her look eerily unreal.

'I wonder if we might have a word,' says the woman. That's exactly what Lauren's form-teacher used to say before she told you off. Why does Lauren feel she's about to be told off again? 'My name is

3

Margaret Curzon,' says the woman. 'And you're Lauren, aren't you?' That gives Lauren a jolt; how does a complete stranger know her name?

'I'm going to be completely honest with you, Lauren,' continues the woman, 'and tell you, straight away, that Roz is a very good friend of mine.' The woman pauses as if she's said something highly significant but Lauren can only stare at her blankly. Who on earth is Roz? The woman's face moves into a huge frown. 'Grant's wife,' she prompts.

'Oh yes, I see,' cries Lauren, covered in embarrassment. Grant's wife, she'd forgotten all about her. Not that she ever knew very much about her, just that she and Grant were separated. She could be here now and Lauren wouldn't recognise her.

'I think the separation hit both Roz and Grant very hard. We were very sad for them, weren't we, Andrew?' She nods at a rather grizzled-looking man, who's been hovering on the edge of their conversation and is currently very busy juggling his chins inside his collar. Either his collar's too tight or he's about to let out one almighty burp. 'Yes, it's always a very difficult time,' she sighs, 'especially when there are children involved. Have you met their son, Royston?'

'No,' says Lauren flatly. She sees what buttons this woman is trying to push. Well, Lauren has nothing to feel guilty about. She's only been seeing Grant, not going out with him. Perhaps she should have that tattooed on her forehead, I'M NOT GOING OUT WITH GRANT.

4

'We're still very close to Roz,' continues the woman and there's no mistaking the ice clinking in her voice now. 'And she needs a lot of support at the moment. When a husband just walks out on you, that takes some adjusting, doesn't it?'

Lauren starts guiltily. So Grant walked out on his wife. She hadn't known that. She'd thought they'd just decided to finish. That was certainly the impression Grant gave her. Not that it's anything to do with Lauren. And really, there's no point in her being told all this, as she's here to finish with Grant. Very soon now, he'll go back to just being her lecturer again.

But the woman is surging on. 'Still, Royston is getting a good deal of support from his friend, Nolan, and Nolan's parents,' and she nods at the couple behind them who are still yarning on to Grant. 'And from Andrew and myself, of course.'

'Well, isn't that just lovely,' says Lauren, unable to stop the sarcasm from bubbling out. 'I'm so very happy for all of you.' Then she stalks off. Horrible woman, trying to make Lauren feel bad. Grant's separation from Roz is absolutely nothing to do with her. But Lauren is still reeling from the discovery that Grant walked out on Roz. What made him do that? No, she just doesn't wish to know.

She starts to walk around the room, clinging on to her now empty glass. In a second she's going over to Grant to tell him she doesn't want to see him any more. But first, she needs to take a few deep breaths.

All around her women exchange pecks on powdery cheeks, while bracelets clink and earrings flash dementedly. A cloud of scent wafts past. That's the wife of the director of the gas board. It was she who'd cut the ribbon to declare Swanks open. She's saying, 'Well, when I heard the builders had let me down again, I was absolutely furious and my husband rang . . .' Another wave of scent and, 'Yes, Ross's headmaster is very pleased with him. We're especially delighted with his science grades. He gained the highest . . .' Imagine going to a party and boasting about exam results. She ought to be thrown out for that.

'Would you like a sandwich?'

'No thanks,' says Lauren, absently.

'Go on, they're free.' It's then Lauren realises she's talking to a girl about her own age, in a black uniform, carrying an enormous tray of salmon sandwiches.

'All right,' says Lauren, grinning.

'Take two,' says the girl. 'You may as well.' The girl looks as if she's about to say something else when a voice proclaims, 'Here come the eats and not before time,' so the girl can only give Lauren a sympathetic look, before being swept away on a sea of outstretched hands.

Lauren has a sudden, mad urge to follow her. A friendly face. The only one. For Lauren doesn't fit in here at all. Even her clothes mark her out as someone different although she'd been convinced there'd be lots of women here in black cocktail dresses. But she's the only one. The alien in the black cocktail dress.

What's rather scary though, is that some of the people here aren't that old, some only about thirty, in fact. In thirteen and a half years time Lauren will be thirty. Will she, then, be going to parties like this and have nothing to talk about other than extensions, her children's exam grades and her latest trip to the garden centre?

She suddenly remembers Jason telling her that on the morning he turns thirty he's going to take poison. He said he'll have it waiting there in a little capsule by his razor. And just as soon as he's opened all his cards . . . Lauren had laughed, of course, and said, when he's thirty he'll be into jazz or something. She kept on teasing him, saying she could see him jogging off to Ronnie Scott's jazz club, and he got so mad . . .

Jason, if only you were here now. Where are you? You'll be out of course, with Tania, when you should be with me. Instead, I'm stuck here. She glares around. None of them want her here. Well, it's mutual. But the closer she tries to get to Jason, the more she finds herself dragged into Grant's life.

Well, it's time Lauren pulled herself out of Grant's life, once and for all. No more waiting around and putting it off. Tell him now. Then she can go home. She pushes her way over to Grant. He's still talking to that couple. He's saying, 'I can tell you where Royston and I ended up but I can't tell you why.' They both laugh politely at this, then the woman suddenly turns round and sees Lauren. Lauren gives her a small smile but the woman's lips don't even quiver upwards; instead, she gives her such an evil stare that Lauren can only gape at her. That woman's acting as if she hates me, thinks Lauren, yet, she doesn't even know me.

Then something snaps inside Lauren. That woman's not so great anyway, in her lime green suit and truly disgusting orange lipstick. And her husband's clearly a prat, his side-burns reach down under his chin. Lauren moves forward, planting herself beside Grant now. 'We wondered where you'd gone,' he says.

'Funny, I didn't think you'd even noticed,' snaps Lauren. She can see the couple looking. Good. They hate her anyway. 'I want to sit down, now,' she demands.

Grant stares at her, looking puzzled and concerned. 'Will you excuse us,' he mutters to the couple but Lauren is already marching away. Grant quickly catches her up and, in fact, over-takes her, as if anxious to show he's still in control. He locates a midget table by the bar which they squash round. Now Grant is looming over her in his mustard-coloured suit, his face looking even longer and thinner than usual.

'Welcome to the adult world,' he drawls.

'What do you mean by that?' she demands.

'This is the adult world you're so eager to see.'

'I didn't want to come here at all,' says Lauren, continuing her rat-bag impression. 'And anyway,

I've been to older people's parties before.' She thinks of her father's parties, which are full of large, sweaty, red-faced men who drink too much, but at least they're friendly and make corny jokes.

'I'm sorry if you felt left out,' says Grant.

Lauren shrugs her shoulders. 'You certainly seemed to be fitting in well,' she says.

Grant looks up. 'They've been very good to Royston. I felt I had to thank them properly.'

No one says anything for a moment and all Lauren can hear is a voice shrieking inside her, 'Tell him now, tell him now.' And then all at once the words pour out. 'Grant, there's something I want to say. I don't think we should see each other any more. I think we should finish tonight.' She sits back, relief flooding through her. At last, she's told him. Now she's gazing down at the table, because she can't look at him. Behind them, someone laughs, a high metallic laugh. Lauren finally lifts up her face. Grant is polishing his glasses. She's never seen him do that before. She almost wishes he would say something now.

But it's then the lights start dimming and spot-lights race around the dance floor below. Then there's a heavy drum-roll and a voice intones, 'Ladies and gentlemen, we are delighted to welcome *The Happy Harrises*. Four men in electric blue suits and one woman in a low cut dress race on to the stage, waving frantically. The lights start to go up again and Grant is saying, quite calmly, 'I know what's happened, they've been at you again, haven't they? Those girls, whose lives are so impoverished, they have to spend all their time gossiping about other people.'

'No,' begins Lauren.

'I'll have a word with them for you.'

'No.'

'What exactly have they been saying?'

'They haven't been saying anything. It's nothing to do with them.'

'So what is the problem then?' She could be back in the classroom being asked to explain an opinion. 'What are you scared of, Lauren?' Then, without waiting for an answer he goes on. 'It hasn't been easy for me either, you know.' His voice rises, just a little, 'I've given up things for you, too.' Then he looks away from her and stares down at one of the *Happy Harrises*, who is yelling jokes into a microphone. Every few seconds little splashes of laughter and clapping break out around them. Still gazing below, Grant says, 'I've already booked tickets for *Jules and Jim* at the Everyman, for next Thursday. It's a film I think you should see. I'll pick you up on Thursday, then,' he says, still not turning round.

'No, no, no,' she cries.

He turns round. 'But you still haven't told me why.' He cracks the last word at her. What can she say, I like you as a lecturer but nothing else? Finally, desperately, 'I want to see other people.'

He stares at her. His lips start turning in against his teeth but he isn't smiling. 'You want to try a few other people out, is that it?' he asks slowly.

10

More than a little wearily now, she says, 'If that's how you want to put it.'

His voice starts to rise. 'Well, isn't your last statement so typical of all you young people. We're all supposed to feel sorry for you, aren't we, the poor, misunderstood adolescent. But what are you really but the most selfish creatures on this earth. You take from everyone and as soon as you're bored with them, as soon as you've used them up, you move on to the next victim. Mercenaries, that's all you are.' He starts stabbing his finger at her. 'Take, take, take.'

'Grant, if I've hurt you, I'm truly . . .'

'Hurt me,' he cries, clenching his fists with frustration. 'Hurt me,' he repeats. Then, all at once, he lunges forward and grabs her wrist.

'Grant, let go,' gasps Lauren at once. She tries to move her hand away but he continues to hold on to her with an extraordinarily powerful grip.

'I've been doing you a favour,' he says, his fingers pressing down harder on to her wrist.

'Let me go,' cries Lauren, 'or I'll scream the room down.' He glares at her, his eyes suddenly tiny, yet burning with anger. Then he releases his grip on her hand as swiftly as he'd grabbed hold of her.

'I can't believe you did that,' gasps Lauren, rubbing her hand. Still breathing heavily, she falls back into her chair. Then she staggers to her feet.

'Where are you going?' he demands.

'Right away from you,' she cries. She blunders away from him, not seeing any of the people she's

11

pushing past, while downstairs a chummy voice is urging everyone to, 'put on your blue suede shoes and rock the night away.'

The band starts to pound away their rendition of *Blue Suede Shoes*. But over the noise she hears a name being called. Her name. It's Grant and he's catching up with her. What should she do? She can't think, only feel anger – and panic. In the end, she lets herself be caught up in the great surge towards the dance floor. But Grant is at her shoulder. 'Lauren, you're being silly, you must let me explain.' He's a teacher again now. I decide when this lesson finishes, not you.

'Get lost.'

'Lauren.'

'Leave me alone. Can you do that?' Just to get away from him she moves on to the dance floor, then looks back. To her great surprise, he isn't behind her anymore. Instead, he's perched right at the edge of the floor. It's then she remembers Grant saying how much he dislikes dancing.

Actually, you can't imagine Grant dancing. He's like those little boys who are so terrified of making a fool of themselves, they never dance or even try and dance, just sit about, making sneering wisecracks. That's Grant. She's right in the middle of the dance floor now. And no, he hasn't moved. He's waiting for her to leave. Then he'll pounce. So she's trapped, isn't she?

She gazes around her. Groups of people are shuffling about the floor, laughing in a half-embarrassed, half-delighted way. Others are already crashing their way back to those days of twisting and jiving with a manic determination. If they dance a bit harder they might even get their old bodies back.

Sometimes at parties, Lauren will hear a piece of music and then just fling herself on to the dance floor, arms flying out in all directions and go totally wild. Grant's never seen her do this, has he? He wouldn't approve at all, would he?

All at once she's flinging off her high-heeled shoes, that's the first thing she always does. Then she half-closes her eyes; as everyone here is at a different party to her, she will have to call up her own atmosphere. Now, watch this, Grant.

She starts moving her head from side to side. Come on, go a bit faster she tells her head. Then she waits for the rest of her body to join in. But nothing happens. Tonight, the circuit is broken. In fact, her legs are growing heavier. All she can do is throw her hair around a bit and sway from side to side.

How weird she must look and what must Grant be thinking? She stifles a giggle. For once in her life, Lauren doesn't care what anyone thinks. She's millions of miles away from them all, anyway. She remembers a girl at a party dancing like this. The girl stared down at the floor all the time, just like Lauren is doing now, and she wore dark glasses. Everyone thought that was most odd. Now it doesn't seem odd at all. Why shouldn't she smear everything with darkness?

For it's only then you can see things, things that

are far away and yet right beside you. Like the time Jason danced with her at that party and then suddenly asked her out. And it was totally unexpected. Only the day before he'd been a sensation on the football pitch – three goals – and Lauren, who hated football, had cheered him madly. But she didn't think he'd really noticed she was there. Then at that party he'd said to her, 'Yesterday you saw me having a bit of a heyday, so now at last I can dare to ask you out.' She'll never forget the way he said that. Or the way she felt so happy, it actually hurt. Everything seemed possible then.

Jason, I want to go back, not twenty years like all these people but just a year and a little bit, back to the beginning. Take me back, please. Her eyes are closed tightly now. And she can actually see him running out of a mist towards her. But now the mist is swallowing him up again, he's gone. And somewhere deep in her throat she lets out a small, dark cry, 'Jason'.

It's then she feels a touch on her hand. Her eyes fly open. She's dreaming standing up. He'll disappear any second. She reaches out to him. He always smells of clean shirts. That's the only way she can describe it. She breathes in his smell then looks up at him. He's dressed entirely in black. He looks like a vigilante. And he's real. HE'S REAL.

'Jason, what are you doing here?'
'Just thought I'd look in.'
'But how did you get in?'
'The usual way.'

14

'But how did you know I'd be . . . Cathy, of course. It was Cathy, wasn't it?'

'I never reveal my sources,' says Jason. Then he adds, 'Are you all right?' and there's such concern in his voice that Lauren has to look away for a second. She doesn't want to cry. Not here.

'Your eyes are amazing,' he says. 'I especially like the green one.' She laughs, and then he kisses her, and the kiss just seems to flow on and on, while he presses her tight against him. Then he whispers something Lauren can't hear.

'Say that again.'

He repeats it but his voice is so low she can still hardly hear him. 'Would you like me to take you home?'

'Yes please,' says Lauren. At once there's a grin on Jason's face so wide it almost splits his face. But he can't have thought Lauren would say, 'No,' surely? She gazes at him in wonderment. There's so much sealed up inside him, perhaps that's what makes him so exciting.

Jason peers around him. 'Look at them all waving their arms about, they look like a field of flipping windmills.' He shakes his head. 'This place is the pits of the earth.' Lauren nods in agreement, then stares down, looking for her shoes.

'My shoes, where have my shoes gone? I took them off when I started dancing.' They both kneel down and peer across the floor. The shoes are nowhere to be seen. 'Maybe they got kicked to the side,' says Jason. But there's no sign of them there

15

either. How embarrassing. 'They can't have just gone,' says Lauren indignantly.

'We'll find them,' says Jason.

Lauren looks up to see Grant striding towards them. 'There's Grant,' she whispers. 'He's also my teacher, so don't . . .'

'Trust me,' says Jason.

Grant is staring right at her. 'I've lost my shoes,' she says lightly.

'You haven't got them, have you?' asks Jason. He adds, 'I'm taking the lady home now.' His tone is polite yet firm. But Grant's eyes remain fixed on Lauren.

'I'm going now, Grant,' says Lauren.

'Are you?' replies Grant. Then he says heavily, 'You do know what you're giving up, don't you?'

Lauren gives him a sad little smile. 'Goodbye, Grant.'

He suddenly screeches after her, 'Well run away then, you stupid little girl. Go on, run away.'

Jason puts his arm around Lauren and starts propelling her to the door. And suddenly, she can't stop trembling. Just seeing him like that unnerved her. But it wasn't her fault, was it?

'Don't look back,' says Jason and Lauren doesn't. As they reach the entrance Jason says, 'That guy is a complete prat and if you want me to go back and . . .'

'No, no.' says Lauren. She takes a couple of deep breaths. 'It's over now. I don't want to see him again, ever.' It's then she realises that she will see Grant again, next week at college. She takes another gulp of air. Why does she feel as if she's been under water for the past few minutes? 'I'm sorry,' she says.

'That's okay. Come and sit down.'

'No, no, I'm all right now.' She gazes down. 'I wouldn't mind my shoes, though.'

'I bet they've been handed in.'

They go over to the cloakroom where a young guy with ginger hair is sitting reading a newspaper.

'Got any shoes?' asks Jason.

'Yes thanks.'

'No, the lady here has lost her shoes.'

'Black high heels,' adds Lauren.

The guy peers over the counter. 'Oh yeah, so she has.' He takes another look. He appears fascinated. Then he says, 'Well, we've had no shoes handed in here, sorry.'

'I'll go and have another look for them,' says Jason. He kisses Lauren on the lips. 'I'll see you shortly.' He turns back, 'And I know your name's not Shortly.' He sprints off while the guy leans conversationally over the counter. 'How did you lose them, then?' She's still talking to him when Jason reappears, shaking his head. 'I reckon that twat Grant has got them. I bet he's going to walk home in them.'

Lauren giggles and says, 'Oh well, if they're gone, they're gone.'

'Leave me your phone number and I can give you a ring if they turn up,' says the guy behind the counter. After doing this, Jason and Lauren walk to the exit.

17

'So what do we do now?'

'It's all under control,' says Jason.

She smiles. 'That's such a Jason phrase, isn't it, it's all under control.'

'I'd planned to have my driver waiting outside.'

'Your driver?'

'Yeah, been with me for years, getting on a bit now, called Samson.'

'Samson,' Lauren starts laughing.

'But like I said, Samson is getting on. So I told him to leave the car at home and I borrowed Adam's motorbike instead.' He points outside – and there, waiting alongside all the massive limos, is one lone motorbike.

'Oh, Jason,' Lauren cries, her voice suddenly muffled. 'You have got it all under control, haven't you?'

'I just had to get you out.'

'Jason's rescue mission,' says Lauren with a teasing smile. Then he says, 'You've got a choice, madam. I can carry you out to your motorbike or you can go piggy-back.'

'Oh, I don't think Samson would approve of me going piggy-back, so . . .'

'I've always wanted to do this,' says Jason and with surprising ease, picks her up. Outside, thin, grey rain is still falling. 'Sorry about the rain,' says Jason.

'What rain?' Lauren says softly. 'I don't see any rain.' Then Jason smiles too, his wonderful wide smile that just takes over his face. He gently places her on the back of the bike.

18

Then he starts to rev the engine up. 'Louder, louder,' cries Lauren. The engine roars and splashes into life and Lauren, clutching tightly on to him now, cries, 'Go, as fast as you can.'

Lauren stirs. She's been dreaming, hasn't she? A dream that's drifting away and she must hold on to it . . . but it's too late. She's floating right away from the dream and up to the surface now. And she so desperately wants to go back, for it was such a beautiful dream. She and Jason had gone back to the hut and . . .

A yellow light is streaming through her curtains. When she was little she used to call this custard time. It's light but too early to get up, time to slip back to . . . but it wasn't a dream – was it?

She sits bolt upright in bed. No, of course it wasn't. It really happened, didn't it? She anxiously runs through last night. Jason carried her out of the awful party because she didn't have any shoes, and then he let her wear his shoes into that late night café while he walked in in his red socks. She laughs out loud, she'll never forget that. And then Jason went to pull one of the pictures off the wall; he said he wanted her to have it as a souvenir. He was desperate she should have a souvenir. She smiles and shakes her head. He's quite mad, of course. Wonderfully, gloriously mad.

And then, he carried her into the hut, back to the beginning. She slides down the bed again. It was there that he said, 'I owe you a massive apology for

19

what I did to you at your fifteenth birthday,' and she said that didn't matter now – and suddenly it didn't. He told her, yes, it was he who'd sent her all the flowers – and then he put his arms around her. She closes her eyes.

And then he stood up and started pacing round the hut. His face was lost in shadow now except for those piercingly blue eyes, which were beamed right on her when he said, 'I should warn you, the damsel the Black Knight rescues is the one he stays faithful to, forever.'

She half-opens her eyes again. But she doesn't want to sleep. What's the point? No dream can match what's happened tonight. She just wants to go on remembering, especially when he said, he'll . . . forever . . . forever.

2
He's Ruining the Best Week of My Life

'Becky, don't say I look rough,' Mark bounces on to a chair opposite her, 'because I've been up all night and I'm still not at all tired.' Becky's never met anyone who gives off so much energy as Mark. He's writhing about on his chair now like someone who's just received a huge electric shock. And he's bursting to tell Becky about last night and, probably, seven million other subjects. All Becky has to do is ask the occasional question – and sit back and listen.

'Last night went well, then?'

'Becky, I can't believe last night. It was just completely amazing.' Mark takes a swig of coffee. It is morning break at Cartford College and the refectory is currently teeming with students. 'Why does the coffee from the machine always have bits floating in it – but cheers for it, anyway.' He puts the paper cup down and pushes away the red metal ashtray which already contains the remains of a thousand cigarettes; the ashtrays seem to be emptied annually.

Then he says, 'Before I went on at the youth club last night, I was so nervous, I tell you, my hands were shaking, everything was shaking. But as soon as I went into *Can't Help Falling in Love* well, you should have seen the girls, Becky, they went wild. It was quite scary. I mean, they wouldn't leave me alone . . . Why are you laughing?'

'I'm not,' says Becky hastily.

'Anyway, the guy who runs the youth club, quite a young guy actually, invited me to this party. I can't remember much about it now. I know there were masses of people there and,' he grins, 'I remember waking up on top of a freezer.'

'That sounds interesting. What were you doing there?'

'Well, they had this freezer in their front room. Can you believe that? And I felt a bit knackered . . . Still, it could have been worse. I might have woken up inside it.' Mark smiles. And every one of his smiles today, provides an excellent view of his tonsils. 'Then, this morning, I found these girls' names and phone numbers all over my jeans. These were the girls who fancied me from the youth club. I only rang one girl up this morning, Vanessa,' he grins mischievously, 'she wrote higher up than anyone else.'

'And?'

'She was out.'

Probably at Infant School, Becky thinks, as the average age of girls who go to that youth club is about nine.

22

'Then, Becky, I'm just going over to the bookshop when Pam Something, from the student union stops me. She said she'd heard about my singing and then, right out of the blue, she asked if I'd be interested in being on the Comic Relief committee.' He gazes impatiently across at Becky. She's not looking stunned enough. 'Me, Becky. Me, who's always been one of life's peasants.'

'No, you haven't,' says Becky, a trifle impatiently.

'I have, Becky,' says Mark solemnly. 'It's a bit different at college but at school, well, there were very definite groups. Like the top people were the lads, they were the kings of the school. Jason was a kind of lad, yet, he was his own person too. Next came the drop-outs, like Jez, who were also respected, in a way.'

'And Adam?'

'No one really knew what Adam was. He kept himself to himself. The lads just left him alone, some people thought he was a bit cool. Then, right at the bottom, you had the peasants, otherwise known as the swots and try-hards. That was what I was, a try-hard.'

'What on earth is that?'

Mark's face tightens. 'A try-hard is someone who tries so hard to be something, he ends up just making himself look stupid. That was me. A joke. A nothing.'

'I think I was a bit like that,' says Becky. 'You know, I'll do this because it looks good and people

23

will like me. They end up just making fun of you. But I've forgotten all that now.'

'I haven't. I still bear grudges.' Then his smile returns. 'But singing at the Karaoke is the best thing I've ever done. Now I'm getting all these offers.'

'Mark – the Karaoke champion of the world,' teases Becky.

'You can laugh.'

'No, I think it's great, Mark. Perhaps, they'll have a Karaoke Olympics.' She starts to laugh again.

Mark's smiling now. 'All right,' he says. 'You'll see one day, when I'm famous, you can say . . .'

'I bought that guy a cup of coffee with bits in it. So where are you next, then?'

He hesitates, for only a second. 'On Tuesday I'm back singing at the youth club again. Come along. Only, come early so you can get a good seat. Then, the following night they've begged me to sing at The Hollybush's Karaoke.' It's funny, Becky thinks, how Mark can say all this without sounding the least bit big-headed. Perhaps, because Mark's confidence can suddenly just ebb away.

'Now, come on, Mark, what's Jason told you about last Friday?'

'Nothing really.' Mark's voice is unexpectedly flat.

'Oh, how disappointing. Its just so strange suddenly seeing them together. It's good though, isn't it?'

'Mmm.'

'This get-together at lunch should be good, shouldn't it?'

24

'Yeah,' then he adds darkly, 'Lauren's already got him well under her thumb.'

'Why do you say that?'

'Because after lunch she's got him going up to London with her to see some crappy French film.'

'What's wrong with that? He just wants to please her.'

'They still leave you in the end,' says Mark with unexpected bitterness. Then he asks, 'Do you reckon Lauren's going to do a runner again?' Earlier in the week Lauren had walked out of the class just before Grant's lesson started. And after break, it is Grant again. But before Becky can reply, Lauren falls on to a chair beside Mark, sighing loudly. Cathy sits down rather more quietly next to Becky.

'I don't believe this place,' exclaims Lauren.

'Why, what's happened?' ask Mark and Becky together.

Lauren sighs again. 'Claire Stallworthy just came up to me and goes, "I suppose you're the best person to ask really, aren't you? Is it true that Grant has chucked you?" '

'And what did you say?' asks Becky.

Lauren shakes her head wearily. 'I said, "Yes, that's right, Claire" and walked off. My minder had a few more words with her.'

'Oh, I just told her to stop making up trouble for people all the time,' says Cathy.

'That Claire Stallworthy is weird,' says Mark. 'She asked me once if it was true that Becky's hair was dyed.'

25

'You never told me that,' exclaims Becky.

'Then another time she asked me if you had any shoes as you only ever wore trainers to college. Don't worry,' Marks adds, 'she only does it because you're really pretty and she's so gross.'

'Oh don't, Mark,' says Cathy. 'If people want to criticise a girl why do they always go on about how ugly she is, or "have you seen her hair." Her looks have got nothing to do with it. She's just one of those people who have to make little digs all the time. It's the only way they can feel better about themselves.'

'No, people just love to see you squirm,' says Mark. 'And once they know they've got to you, well, they go on even more then.'

'Most people are all right,' says Cathy. 'It's just a few who have to stir things up. That's why I think if Lauren goes to Grant's lesson as usual it will stop the gossip.'

'Yes, it might,' says Becky.

Lauren doesn't reply. She looks pale and tense, as if she's about to go and do an exam she hasn't revised for. Around them the clatter of cups is starting to die down; the exodus back to the classroom is under way.

'I suppose we'd better go,' says Cathy. 'We don't want to go into Grant's lesson late, do we, Lauren?'

'You go, I'll stay in this nice, freezing cold canteen and pretend I never went up to Grant that night at Charades, pretend I never saw him, pretend he's not ruining the best week of my life.'

'But it's over now, Lauren. You've finished with

him. He'll go back to being just your teacher now,' cries Cathy.

'But will he, though? You didn't see his eyes when I tried to finish with him or the way he grabbed . . .'

'He's not going to do anything in the classroom, though, is he? He's got his reputation to consider, hasn't he?' Cathy turns to Becky and Mark, who murmur support. Cathy goes on, 'And you've worked so hard on this latest essay just so you can show them you can get an A without any, what Claire Stallworthy would call, "foul-play".'

'Yes, but Cathy, what if he does say something? It's bad enough now with everyone whispering and gossiping about me, without anything else.' There's an unfamiliar crack in her voice as Lauren says this. 'I feel as if I've fallen down a deep well and the more I try and pull myself out the deeper I go down . . .'

'No, you pulled yourself out last Friday,' says Cathy. 'You're out and you've got Jason back and in a couple of hours we're all going out for lunch . . .'

'I know, and Grant's even casting a shadow over that.'

'I think you're making too much of him,' says Cathy. 'I really do. It's over and he can't do anything.' Her words hang in the air while around them the kitchen staff are collecting up cups and muttering over the mess.

'Come on, Lauren,' says Cathy. Mark and Becky stand up.

'You go then,' says Lauren. 'I'm sorry, I just can't face him.'

27

Mark sits down again. 'Lauren,' he says solemnly, 'even if Grant does say something, even if Grant does humiliate you, will it really matter? In ten years time will you even remember who he is? Will any of us? Who knows, we might all just be food for worms then. One day that's how we'll end up – worm food.' He leans forward. 'Sometimes I find that thought oddly comforting. It makes me braver somehow.' Lauren's eyes come up slowly and she stares hard at Mark for a couple of seconds. Then she gives her familiar throaty laugh.

The class gasp in astonishment. Grant is switching on the overhead projector. If he'd walked in wearing a mortar-board and gown the class couldn't have been more shocked.

'I'd like you to copy down these notes on the ending of *Hard Times*.' The class stare at him incredulously, while Grant stares at nothing.

'Boring,' mutters a voice. Now there's a word that hasn't been heard in one of Grant's lessons before – and Grant flinches, just a little, before saying, 'As you copy the notes down you might like to think about the difference between endings in fiction and in real life. Namely, in real life there can be no happy endings, only delayed unhappy ones.' He adds, 'There are two more pages of notes after this one, so you'd better get a move on.' Then he goes and sits behind his desk, while bags are reluctantly opened and pens and notepads slammed on to the desks.

'I haven't got any paper, Grant,' says a voice from the back.

'Borrow some.' Suddenly, Grant is sounding just like an ordinary lecturer. The class don't like it.

Another voice. 'Grant, are you in a mood with us?' There's a sudden hush before Grant drawls, 'I don't think that question merits an answer, do you? Now, you have a lot of work to do.'

Then, a piercingly loud whisper, 'No, he's not in a mood with US.'

Lauren gives a little shiver. Cathy whispers, 'Ignore them – and him – if he wants to act like a sulky nine-year-old, let him.' Her voice is unexpectedly harsh. And Lauren thinks how strange it is that Cathy, who feels obliged to give money to every beggar in London and is just about the most compassionate person she knows, cannot summon up the tiniest measure of pity for Grant. Lauren can. Downstairs in the canteen she had just hated him. He wasn't a person then, only an evil force casting giant shadows over every corner of her life. And if in the classroom he'd sat glaring at her or had tried to humiliate her, well, in a way, she'd have preferred it. But now, she's forced to see, not a dark force but a man who can't make eye contact with her, with anyone.

There's something behind his eyes he doesn't want anyone else to see. But Lauren knows what's there. Hadn't she felt the same deep agonising pain after she and Jason had broken up? And she'd guarded it just as fiercely. That's why, even a year

29

later at Charades, she still couldn't face Jason and had run away, straight into Grant.

Now it's Grant who's suffering because of her. It's his own fault, of course. He was way out of order at Swanks. He was like a madman. Still, Lauren can afford to be a little generous now. It's then she decides she'll write him a message at the end of her essay; that at least will give him a little dignity. And it will end things in a rather more civilised way than him yelling things at her as she ran out of Swanks.

'Right, I'm moving on to the second page of notes now,' says Grant. There are groans and cries of 'NOT YET!'

'You've had plenty of time,' says Grant. Mark asks Becky, 'Can I copy your last two lines?' Then he gazes at her in astonishment. 'You've hardly written anything,' he says.

'I know. I just can't concentrate.'

'What are you doing, dreaming about me?'

'How did you guess?'

'You only saw him last night, didn't you?'

'Yes.'

'You have got it bad.'

Becky can feel herself turning red. 'I'm just bored, that's all.'

Mark hunches his shoulders, then says, 'Some of us have got work to do,' and turns away. Becky can't help feeling embarrassed. It's awful really, isn't it? Right now, all she can think about is Adam. It's scary too, someone having all that power over your thoughts.

Last night Adam rang her from a call box and immediately she panicked, thinking his mum had said something about seeing Becky and Adam hugging. But she hadn't and Adam had just wanted to talk to her. Then he suggested meeting up in the park for a few minutes.

They stopped off at this café where they bought these cartons of milk shakes. Only Adam's exploded all over him. His shirt and trousers were just covered in the stuff. And he just laughed, as if to say, it's no big deal. He wasn't self-conscious about it at all. And although it was just a tiny incident, Becky really admired him for that.

It's funny really, Adam's not a great poseur like Jason. You notice him almost despite himself. Yet, he has got a style all of his own and you find yourself thinking about something he said or did.

Actually, when she got home last night she intended doing some background reading for her *Hard Times* essay. And she'd sat there reading these books she'd got from the library and not taking in a word . . . the lines just flashed by, like scenery from a speeding train. All she could think about was Adam.

Yet, she'd been going out with him for over a month now. Normally that's when you start to take each other for granted and become a bit restless. She remembered this boy who used to ring her up every night and after a couple of weeks she dreaded it. But this time, she and Adam could just chat away for hours, quizzing each other about the silliest things. And yet, there's still more and more to know. In a way, the closer you get to someone the more mysterious they become. That's certainly true of Adam.

Mark frowns. 'You're going to have yards of notes to copy out, you know.' Becky nods solemnly. But right now, she couldn't care less. All she can think about is this impatient fluttering in her stomach.

Lauren looks down at what she's written: Grant, I feel badly about how it ended. Thank you for all the interesting visits. I know you have put yourself out for me. Best of luck in the future. Lauren.

It's taken her ages to compose this little apology and she's still not sure about it, especially the "best of luck in the future" bit. Does that sound silly? But she can't just write, "Yours sincerely". Or, on the other hand, she doesn't want to put "love".

'Right, that's it.' Grant switches off the overhead projector. 'Leave your essays on my desk before you go. No excuses accepted or believed.' He slumps down into his chair again, his whole body language saying, don't talk to me.

Lauren gets up and as casually as she can, walks up to Grant's desk. She can feel Cathy's eyes burning into her as she approaches his desk. Some of the students turn and watch too. Lauren picks up the pile of essays and slips hers into the middle. She always does that, never leaves her essay on the top. Grant teased her about that once. Today, he doesn't seem to have noticed her. But at least he will see her note and that will help, won't it?

She turns round to see Cathy, Becky and Mark waiting for her. Lauren instinctively takes charge.

'So what are we doing? Cathy and I have got to get some money out, so do you want to go ahead?'

'Becky does,' says Mark with a grim smile. 'She's just panting with excitement at the thought of seeing Adam, after being parted from him for a whole . . .'

'Actually,' interrupts Becky, 'Adam's got a practical this morning so he won't be finished for another twenty minutes yet.'

Mark looks up. 'So it's just you and me, then. Becky, can you bear it?'

Becky laughs and takes his arm. 'I'll be brave,' she says.

All that's missing in here, thinks Adam, is a stuffed zebra. This is "Two Tone", a restaurant devoted to black and white '60s style and he is reclining in a booth, over which hangs the sign THE KINGS ROAD. Elsewhere, there is CARNABY STREET, SLOANE SQUARE and beside what is clearly the top table, ABBEY ROAD, alongside which is a huge blow-up photograph of The Beatles, on that zebra crossing.

All over the restaurant are large black and white photographs of girls with beehive hairdos and rather intense looking boys, none of whom Adam recognises, while '60s songs are endlessly played. And all the staff are in black and white uniforms; the guy at the door even had one of those naff piano ties on.

This could be a really happening place, if only everyone here wasn't so serious about it all. The two couples on the Abbey Road table for instance, who seem to be drinking glasses of phlegm with trees growing out of them, just look so self-conscious, not relaxed at all. It's supposed to be better in the evenings when the customers dress up.

'Are you all right?' Adam looks up. Why does the waitress's tone suggest he's definitely not all right?

'Yes, fine,' says Adam. 'I'm still waiting for my friends. They are coming. It's just I'm a bit early.' Like an hour.

She nods at his empty glass and then gives him a hard stare. Adam feels as if she's just peeked inside his wallet and isn't too impressed by the four pounds, four pence she's found there. That's why Adam isn't ordering any more drinks. 'They'll be here any minute now,' says Adam. She stomps off. But even the back of her neck has a suspicious air about it.

Bet she's never had a customer before who's sat here for an hour and ten minutes and drunk just one half of lager. The reason he's been here so long is that he never actually made his human biology class this morning. He was half an hour late and he just couldn't face the interrogation. He hates having to make excuses, even if the reasons are genuine. And today he had no excuse, not one he could recite to his lecturer anyway. Plus, he hasn't done this week's homework. Or last week's. He was going to sit in the library and catch up there. But instead, he wandered round the town and generally wasted time. Still, one good thing happened. He passed the local garage, saw they were advertising for someone and, on impulse, applied. To his total astonishment, he got the job. They've given him all the unsocial hours of course, but he doesn't mind. He'll be earning money (quite good money, too) and it'll be a good excuse for him to get out of the house whenever he wants.

Then Adam hears a voice saying, 'One of your party has already arrived; and Mark and Becky rush into view.

'What are you doing here?' demands Mark.

'I didn't go in today,' says Adam. Becky immediately slides beside him. 'We were doing bones today,' adds Adam.

'That sounds absolutely fascinating,' smiles Becky.

'Oh, it is. Look at this bone, now draw it, now read those two thousand hand-outs.'

'So you've been dossing about Cartford instead,' says Mark, sitting opposite them.

'Yeah, well, Cartford's just such an exciting place to be,' says Adam. 'Still, got myself a job.'

'Where?' demands Mark.

'At Bailey's garage, start this Sunday.'

Becky lightly touches his hand and immediately he clasps it tightly. They're off, thinks Mark. How inconsiderate can they get? Don't they know they're making him feel a right twat? He hasn't even got a glass to stare into. Any second now they'll probably start snogging.

What makes it worse is that Becky is looking particularly attractive. Her eyes are a very bright green today and her red hair is positively shining, while her skin is just calling out to be kissed . . . He sighs loudly. They don't even hear him. He stares up at the faces on the wall. 'Well just look at the lips on that one . . .' Then he adds, 'Sorry to interrupt you, just thought I'd try and get back into this conversation.' And there's such a pained expression on his face as he says this that Becky starts guiltily. She and Adam unclasp hands.

Adam asks, 'So where's everyone else?'

'They're just getting some money,' says Becky. 'They won't be long.' (Adam can't help feeling relieved about that.)

'It's quite dark in here, isn't it?' says Becky conversationally.

'That's so you can't see what you're eating,' replies Mark. 'Even the menus are in black and white. You don't suppose the food will be black and white, do you? Here, have a menu, Becky.'

'Thanks, Mark.'

'Just look on me as the prop man,' he mutters. And Becky can't decide if Mark is really in a mood or just pretending. Mark offers a menu to Adam.

'No, it's okay mate, I've already seen it and I've picked what I'm having – pasta da luncha.'

'Oh, where's that?' asks Becky. 'That sounds quite nice. It always takes me ages to decide what to have.'

Mark says, 'Well don't try ordering anything with meat in it, not with Cathy around.' He starts reading his menu, then calls out, 'Scratch and Peck. Imagine saying to the waitress, I'll have a Scratch and Peck,' he starts laughing.

'What exactly is a Scratch and Peck?' asks Becky.

'Adam will show you tonight,' says Mark, laughing really loudly now.

The waitress materialises into view. 'Are you ready to order?'

'No, we've still got three friends to come. They're getting the money.' He tries a small smile. The waitress doesn't respond.

'Do you want to order drinks?' asks the waitress.

Adam shakes his head.

'I'll just have an orange and lemonade,' says Becky.

'And I'll have a lager please,' says Mark. 'A pint.'

'Have you any ID?' asks the waitress.

Mark is stunned. 'What?'

'Any ID, to prove you are eighteen.'

Mark gazes at her furiously. 'I don't need to carry ID. I'm twenty, aren't I?'

'Yes, he is,' says Adam fervently.

'He's never been asked before,' says Becky.

'I'm sorry, but unless you carry ID I can't serve you alcohol.'

'Why?' demands Mark.

The waitress's tone is barely polite now. 'Because we are not allowed to serve alcohol to anyone who looks under-age.' She turns away.

'But I'm twenty,' screams Mark. 'You can ring up my mum if you like. Cartford 437711. Go on, ring

37

her. She'll tell you . . .' But the waitress doesn't even turn round.

'Here's one,' says Jason, getting up. Everyone puts their coffee cups down and leans forward again. 'And it's true too. This woman was stopped by an old geezer who lived down her road and he asked her if she liked Brazil nuts, only he's been given a whole bag full but couldn't eat them because of his false teeth. So she told him that she did like Brazil nuts and took the bag and ate them all. A few days later she saw him again and said, "Thanks ever so much for the Brazil nuts." "That's all right, my dear," the old geezer replied. "Once I've sucked the chocolate off they're no good to me!" '

Everyone, but Mark, erupts into laughter and exclamations of horror. Then Mark starts laughing too. 'He's just worked it out,' says Cathy.

Mark gets up. 'Got some jokes for you,' he says. 'Why does the monkey fall out of the tree?'

'Because it's dead,' says Adam.

'Yeah, that's right,' says Mark. 'But why did the second monkey fall out of the tree?' and, before anyone can answer, he says, 'because it was sello-taped to the first one.' There are groans and cries of 'Mark, that's awful!' 'All right, there's this three-legged chicken . . .' 'Heard it,' cries everyone. Mark falls down in his chair again. 'Here, have some more lager,' says Jason, pouring a generous portion of his lager into Mark's glass.

Then Cathy stands up. 'I'd like to propose a toast,'

she says. 'I meant to do it earlier but, well, I didn't . . . anyway, I think you can guess who the toast is for. It's exactly one week ago tonight that Jason walked into Swanks . . .'

'Walked,' cries Jason in mock indignation. 'Don't you mean cruised?'

Cathy smiles. 'Sorry, since Jason cruised into Swanks, searching around for Lauren.'

'Did you spot her right away?' asks Becky.

'Oh yeah,' says Jason, 'she just stood out, like a penguin in a bathing suit.'

Lauren laughs. 'He's such a little flatterer.'

'And Lauren, how did you feel when you first saw Jason?' asks Becky.

Lauren gives one of her unexpectedly shy smiles, 'Oh, you know.'

'No, come on, tell us. We want to know, don't we?' says Becky.

'When I saw Jason, I thought, what on earth's he doing here,' says Lauren.

'And?' prompts Becky.

'And I felt just amazingly happy,' says Lauren quickly.

Mark gives a loud yawn. 'Sorry, but I'm wrecked. By the way, did you ever get your shoes back, Lauren?'

'No, Mark, I never did.'

'I told you,' says Jason, 'Grant nicked them. He's probably sitting at home stroking them now.'

'I'd just like to add,' says Cathy, 'that Lauren's had a few hassles in her life recently, not least her

39

dad going up to college on Monday and sorting out the Principal.'

Lauren smiles. Still, at least her dad made sure that the incident about the library books was closed. And that was good of him. But all the time her dad was in college she'd been absolutely terrified he was going to see Grant. Thank goodness they never met. She never wants her dad to find out about her and Grant.

'But,' continues Cathy, 'all that is behind her now. And I think, we all think, that Lauren and Jason belong together and this time, well, they'd better not mess it up again. So raise your glasses please, to Lauren and Jason.' Adam, Becky and Mark stand up and join Cathy in toasting Lauren and Jason, who look both embarrassed and pleased.

Then Lauren gets up, 'I'd like to propose a toast, to Cathy, because she helped to plot last Friday – behind my back, too,' she gives a wry smile, 'and for being the best friend in the world and because we all missed her birthday last week, though we are going to make up for it by buying her some amazing presents – and you're not paying a penny towards this meal . . . Everyone, Cathy.' Cathy's name echoes round the table and glasses are solemnly clinked.

Cathy, whose neck has turned a bright red, says, 'I wasn't expecting that. Thanks.' As she smiles around at everyone, Lauren thinks how incredibly young she suddenly looks, like a little girl who still believes in Father Christmas. 'Actually, I was so pleased you forgot my birthday, as I find birthdays really depressing, you know, another year gone that you can never get back. But,' she grins mischieviously, 'this year I did something on my birthday I've never done before.'

'I knew I shouldn't have given you those hand-cuffs,' says Mark.

'Ignore him,' laughs Becky. 'Come on, Cathy, what did you do?'

'Well, I went out and had my first driving lesson.'

'You never told me about this,' says Lauren.

'No, well I'd got my provisional licence and then I thought, why not. I've only had one lesson so far with this guy who's about ninety and wears a hat and scarf all the time.'

'Did you actually drive?' asks Lauren.

'Well, first of all he went through the gears, the clutch, all that stuff, then he handed me this round tin tray and told me to put my hands on the side and the top. We were ages messing about with this tray. And then he says to me, "Right, now drive." Well, I went down the road at about five miles an hour and he kept saying something about the clutch and patting my knees . . . I'm wearing jeans in future.'

'I've put in for my test already,' announces Jason.

'But you're not even seventeen yet,' says Cathy.

'Yeah, but it's just a formality,' says Jason airily. 'I've got it pretty well sussed. Going to get a car of my own, any day now.'

'I reckon it's going to take me months and months to learn,' says Cathy. 'There's just so much to remember. Still, if I could drive, it would be good.

41

Next time Giles bugged me I could just dive into my car . . .'

'Giles being a pain, then?' asks Becky.

'We just don't get on,' says Cathy, 'and I don't think we ever will.'

A saucer is slapped down on the table. A saucer containing the bill.

'Do you think that's a hint?' says Adam, picking up the bill.

Lauren is still staring after the waitress. 'Just what is her problem, thumping the bill down like that? She's a disgrace. It's because we're young and don't fit in with their image of this place. She ought to be reported.' Mark nods vigorously in agreement.

'So what's the damage, Adam?' asks Jason.

'Fifty-eight pounds, and seventy-four pence,' reads Adam. 'Not too bad. What's that divided by six – no, five?'

'I don't mind paying,' says Cathy.

'No, Cathy, put your money away,' says Lauren. 'If we each put twelve pounds in.'

'I hate to ask,' says Adam, 'but I don't suppose anyone could lend me a tenner, could they? Now I've got a job I can pay them back . . .'

'I will,' interrupts Mark. 'No prob,' and he tosses a ten pound note into the saucer. 'I'm making big money now.'

'Thanks, mate. I'll pay you back on Sunday.'

'No rush,' says Mark.

As the saucer goes round, Adam says, 'You know, I wouldn't mind owning a restaurant one day, only it'd be on the roof of a museum, like the one James Dean used to go to. And it'd be for musicians and writers and actors, a place where they could relax.'

'And no-one asked for ID,' interrupts Mark. 'Can I take the money up to her? I want to give her a really dirty look.'

'Hold on,' cries Cathy, jumping up, 'I want to take a photograph of you all first, for Jez.'

'Have you heard from him lately?' asks Adam.

'Just a postcard, on my birthday, actually. I was surprised. He's promised me a letter.'

'Cathy,' says Lauren, 'I hate to tell you, but you've got a dirty great stain on your dress.'

'Yeah, I know,' says Cathy, 'I can't get rid of it. I sat on some salad cream last summer and . . . All right everyone, bunch in now.'

'Are you sure you don't want me to take it?' says Becky. 'Then you can have all the original gang.'

'Don't be silly,' says Mark at once. 'You're one of us now – isn't she?' Cathy and Adam nod vigorously and even Lauren murmurs in agreement. Becky can't help feel a stab of pride. She feels as if she's been accepted into a most exclusive club.

'All right everyone,' cries Cathy. 'Adam, get down a bit, that's better. All right. Here goes.'

The flash goes off and Mark declares, 'I blinked. I always blink.'

'Will you get me a copy of that picture, Cathy?' asks Lauren.

'And me,' says Becky.

Jason looks at his watch. 'I suppose we'd better go

if we're not going to miss the start of this amazing French film. What's it called – *Julie and Johnnie*.'

'*Jules et Jim*,' corrects Lauren.

'I just don't see,' says Jason, 'how you can watch a film and read sub-titles at the same time.'

'Of course you can,' cries Lauren. 'Can't you, Cathy?'

Cathy doesn't answer at first. Then she says, 'Well, as it happens, I'm not going.'

'But why?' demands Lauren.

'Oh, I thought I'd just stay in, do a few things.'

'What things?'

Before Cathy can answer, Mark is saying, 'You don't want to play gooseberry, do you, Cathy, and I don't blame you.'

'Well, no,' begins Cathy. But Lauren is already declaring, 'Cathy, you must come. I mean, this is our trip. I've only brought Jason along to protect us on the train home.' Then Jason joins in, and everyone's calling things out and Cathy's wishing she hadn't said anything. Especially as it isn't that she's afraid of playing gooseberry – well, not really – she'd just thought it would be a nice gesture freeing Jason and Lauren to go off on their own. But instead it's all got blown up.

Finally, Mark and Adam go and settle the bill, Lauren and Becky disappear to the ladies but Jason is still staring intently at Cathy, 'So you are coming to see . . . what's its face?'

'*Jules and Jim*,' says Cathy. 'Yes, all right.'

44

'Because if I've got to watch this film, then so have you. You're not getting out of it that easily.'

Cathy's smiling just a little wearily. Jason's meaning to be kind. Everyone is. So why does that make her feel worse, like some kind of little orphan? 'I just thought you and Lauren might like some time on your own.'

'No, not really,' says Jason, grinning.

'Sick of her already, are you?' teases Cathy. Then she says, 'Still, it's finally happened, you and Lauren going out together again. I was surprised it wasn't on the news actually. You must feel really good, Jason.'

'My face just can't stop smiling,' but then he says, 'it's scarey too, though.'

'How's that?'

'You've got something to lose, haven't you?'

'You won't lose Lauren again,' says Cathy firmly.

Jason picks up his coffee spoon and absently taps it on the table. 'And then going out – is a bit dodgy – isn't it?'

'How come?' Cathy leans forward, fascinated. Jason hardly ever talks about things like this.

'Well, going out with someone,' he smiles, 'that's the ultimate open-up, isn't it?'

'Yes, I suppose it is really.' She thinks about this. 'But what are you worried about, with your amazing good looks?'

He grins broadly. 'Yes, you're right.'

'And your great charm.'

Jason nods again, but then says, with unexpected seriousness, 'But my charm's a very short-lived thing.' Before he can say anything else Mark and Adam are back and Jason's acting, well, like Jason again. But all the way to London, Cathy's thinking about what he said. What a strange thing to say, "my charm is a very short-lived thing." And it's not true either. So why did he say it?

The words are swimming before Lauren's eyes. She just can't believe it. But there's no mistake. She looks away. But Grant's comments are still pounding away in her head: *Is this the best you can do? Maybe you've been out all night. I cannot think of any other explanation for such an appalling essay.* While in the margin waits Grant's handgrenade; a giant E.

Cathy nudges her. 'I got a B. For the first time Grant's given me a B. What did you get, another A, I suppose?

Without a word Lauren hands her essay over to Cathy. 'An E!' exclaims Cathy. Then she reads his comments. 'But that's outrageous – and what's all this he's crossed out?'

'I wrote him a message,' says Lauren. 'I thought it might help. Instead, he's torn a hole in the paper.'

'But he's gone crazy,' says Cathy. 'Well, he's not getting away with this.'

3 *Jason's Solution*

Lauren throws her essay on Grant's desk. 'You gave me an E – I want to know why.' He doesn't say anything, just slowly picks up the essay.

She glances around the empty classroom, then over at the door where Cathy, Mark and Becky are waiting outside, their faces pressed right up against the glass. They see her and give her the thumbs up. How funny they look, like naughty children who've been sent out. Actually, half-way through the lesson Grant nearly did send all four of them out. They were whispering together about (what else?) Lauren's essay grade, when he suddenly snapped, 'Would you four prefer to leave now, then you can carry on your conversation without disturbing everyone else.' Then he turned to the class, that unmistakable glint of triumph in his eyes. While all around her, Lauren could see little gloating smiles.

Grant stares hard at her essay for at least half-a-second. 'I believe I have explained my reasons for the grade on your paper.'

'But I didn't understand what you meant.'

'I see. What I meant was that your essay felt rushed, it lacked judgement and your usual . . . maturity.' Grant's tone is icily polite but smug as hell, too. It's as if he's saying, I've shown you, haven't I? Now you know just how powerful I can be.

He picks her essay up and waves it at her. 'I'm sorry you were disappointed,' he says, 'but please remember I was also disappointed in you, Lauren.' His voice softens ever so slightly when he says her name.

'The little message I wrote to you. You crossed it all out.'

He drops the essay. 'Were you really surprised that I did?'

Lauren's leaning over his desk now. Go on. Face up to him. What's she got to lose? 'Yes, I was.'

His face tightens sharply. 'You women, at heart you're all cowards, aren't you? My wife can't tell me she wants a divorce. She has to write me a note . . .'

'But that's what you wanted, wasn't it – a divorce?' interrupts Lauren.

He doesn't reply, just makes a strange noise in his throat as if he were fighting to control himself. 'We've only been separated a short time and already she thinks she's found someone else.'

Lauren stares at him contemptuously. What does he expect his wife to do; sit crying into her pillow over him every night? Yes, that's exactly what he wants – while he goes off and enjoys himself.

'Women, you can't trust any of them,' he mutters, more to himself than to Lauren. Then he declares, 'I've been good to you and this is how you re-pay me, brushing me off as if I'm some lovesick adolescent admirer of yours, with this two-line note.'

'If I . . .'

'I!' he hurls the word back at her, 'that's your favourite word, isn't it, Lauren? A few jealous girls make some comments and you have to throw everything away.' How many times does Lauren have to tell him that's not the reason she ended it? 'Well, you're not the only one who has to put up with abuse, you know.' Out of his rucksack, he pulls out his file. Then, from the front of the file he produces a chewing-gum wrapper. 'This was thrown on to my desk by one of your classmates. Go on, read it.'

Lauren takes the wrapper, undoes it and then sees in large red capitals, GRANT, PLEASE COME BACK TO ME. I MISS YOU SO MUCH. LOVE LAUREN XXXXXX.

Lauren stifles a smile. It's so obviously a fake, that it's not even worth bothering about. She's amazed Grant didn't just throw it in the bin. But instead, he takes the wrapper from her and places it in front of his file, where she sees he's still kept all the birthday cards the students gave him, even though that is now over a month ago. She suddenly thinks of an old aunt of hers (actually, a great-aunt) who used to keep her birthday cards up all year, or so it seemed. And whenever you visited her, she'd beg you not to go. Often she'd cry when you did leave. And Lauren would stand there with her mum, thinking what an embarrassing woman this is. Really, she was just deeply lonely. For a moment, Lauren actually feels a flicker of sympathy for Grant.

But as soon as he starts talking again, the sympathy evaporates for he's doing his 'I'm so hard done by' act again and Lauren is fed up with it. He's saying, 'Do you think I liked finding that wrapper on my desk and being reduced to a joke? Well I didn't. I am your lecturer and entitled to respect. See what I put up with for you?'

Lauren doesn't really think a silly message on a chewing-gum wrapper is any big deal. Somewhat impatiently now she says, 'Will you please re-mark my essay?'

He leans back in his chair. 'No, I won't,' he says. 'You were doing very well.' He pauses. 'You could do well again.' The suggestion hangs in the air while Lauren gazes at him in horror. It's hard to believe she ever liked him now. And to think she respected his maturity. Now she can't think of anyone she hates more. She wouldn't be surprised if he hated her, too. She's sure he doesn't really want to go out with her again. Now it's all just a power game to him, isn't it?

'I'd rather fail,' Lauren hisses, before snatching up her essay. 'By the way, you won't mind if I ask another lecturer to look at this essay, will you?' Earlier she'd thought of saying this – well, Mark suggested it actually – but then rejected it as being too snidey. Now she has no such scruples.

His tiny dark eyes, which look as if they are all pupil, stare right at her. Is there a hint of sadness in those eyes? Does it hurt him just a little to realise how much she hates him now? But then he gives a harsh little laugh. 'No, I don't mind at all – just as you won't mind me having a word with your father, will you?'

'We're just not happy about it.' Lauren's mum puts the cups on the silver tray. 'Does he take sugar?'

'Four spoonfuls,' says Lauren.

'Good gracious, that's very bad for him.' She puts the sugar bowl on the tray. 'No, we're both very concerned.'

'But, Mum, there's no need, honestly,' says Lauren.

'You can't blame us for being worried,' booms her dad from the kitchen doorway. She stares at him in surprise. For her dad's taken off the suit which he practically lives in during the week and is wearing his new cords and a polo-neck jumper. He says, 'I wanted to show your young man that we're very casual and easy-going here, and also that sometimes people our age can still dress in the fashion.' Actually, cords are deeply unfashionable (well they are in Cartford, anyway) but Lauren doesn't say anything.

He continues, 'It's just your mother and I remember what happened the last time you went out with this . . . Jason. And the way he took the legs from under you.' He puts an arm around her. 'And I don't ever want to see my girl hurt.' Lauren squeezes his arm. She's always been Daddy's girl and even now she'd hate to do anything to disappoint him. That's why she never wants her father to find out about Grant. For her father, for all his funny little ways, trusts Lauren. Yet, if he found out about Grant, well, he'd start to think all kinds of things which weren't true. But how could she explain it to him? It's hard enough explaining it to herself.

Just why did she go out with Grant . . . ? How often has she asked herself that? Well, it was flattering, of course, that was part of it, but also when she and Grant went to Lombards, on their first so-called date . . . Well, none of it seemed real. Certainly, to Lauren it didn't. The whole evening was just a little holiday from her real life. Some holiday!

And now, what is she to do about Grant? Cathy thinks she should call his bluff and show the essay to another lecturer. She says Grant wouldn't dare contact Lauren's dad, it would be too embarrassing for him. But Lauren isn't so sure. At the moment it's really hard to know what Grant will do.

'Don't look so worried,' says her dad. 'If this lad is good to you, I'll be good to him, that's the way I am.'

'Your father's always fair,' adds her mother, loyally. A couple of weeks ago Dad replaced Mum's Mercedes sports car with an old banger – that was her punishment for putting on weight. Well, for once, Mum got really mad with him. Dad immediately said it was a joke, brought the Mercedes back, filled every room with flowers, took her out for a meal in London and now they're a double-act again.

'Your father will give Jason every chance,' continues her mum. This sounds a bit ominous to Lauren. She says, 'Don't forget, Jason's coming round for a cup of tea, not a major interrogation.' Lauren has vivid memories of past boyfriends cowering down in their chair while her father fired questions at them.

'I remember this Jason as a good-looking boy,' muses her mum, 'but I always thought he was rather immature. I mean, one time he was sitting down at this kitchen table with you when he started unbuttoning his shirt.'

Lauren laughs. 'Oh, Mum, that was just a joke,' she says, 'and that was years and years ago.' They can't have been more than . . . that's right . . . they were eleven. For the week before she'd gone to a party, well actually, it was just a group of kids sitting in someone's front room, with a bottle of cider and four cans of lager. But Lauren was in the middle of it all, plastered with make-up, when Jason came up to her and said, 'I heard you were pretty,' then he gave a goofy smile and added, 'and all the rumours are true.' And that was the first time they really spoke. She gives a little romantic sigh.

The doorbell ringing hurtles Lauren into the present again.

'We'll go and sit in the sitting room,' says her mum, 'just make everything look natural.'

'And be nice, please,' hisses Lauren.

'Just remember, Lauren,' says her father gravely, 'we've got your best interests at heart.'

Lauren rushes to the door. Then, she lets out a low gasp when she sees Jason. He's wearing a white shirt, dark brown trousers, a brown tie . . . he could be going for a job interview. Even his shoes are gleaming.

'You look smart,' she says.

'Good evening, Lauren,' he says, so politely she nearly cracks up. But of course, Jason is playing a part and, she suspects, is enjoying himself greatly.

'Come in and say hello to my mum and dad,' she says.

'Certainly,' he replies.

Inside the sitting room, Mum and Dad are standing talking together in a most unnatural pose.

'Mum, Dad, here's Jason to say hello.'

Lauren's mum comes forward. 'Ah, welcome, Jason, good to see you again.'

Suddenly, Jason looks so tall, positively towering over her mum. He vigorously shakes her hand. 'And it's good to see you again, Eileen.' Her mum starts, both at the warmth of his handshake and the way he's used her first name. 'These are for you, Eileen,' he says, taking a pound box of chocolates from under his arm.

'Oh, how kind,' she mumbles.

'And this of course is Bill,' says Jason, advancing towards Lauren's dad, hand outstretched. 'Good to see you again.' Even her father can only stare at this

Mr Confidence, and they exchange handshakes in silence. 'Don't mind if I sit down, do you, Bill? Thanks,' says Jason, slumping right back in his chair, seemingly totally at ease.

'I've just made some tea,' says Lauren's mum. 'Would you care for some, Jason?'

'That would be very nice. Thank you,' says Jason. 'By the way, Eileen,' Lauren's mum turns round, 'I do like the way you've done your hair. It really suits you.'

'Oh, thank you,' cries her mum, both pleased and flustered by this unexpected compliment.

Then Jason turns to Lauren's dad, who still appears to be in a state of shock. 'Well, Bill, so how's business?'

'Yo, there's me,' Jason sounds genuinely surprised. His eyes rove around Lauren's bedroom. 'And here's another one. You got that out of the newspaper, didn't you?' He grins over at Lauren who is sprawled across her bed. 'And will you look at the way I'm waving that swimming trophy about – what a little poseur.'

'Haven't changed much, have you?' Lauren gives a wicked laugh. 'Still the biggest poseur in Cartford.'

Jason strolls over to her, grinning broadly. 'Such a slur on my character demands revenge,' and all at once he's grabbing her right foot and tickling it.

'No, Jason, don't!' Lauren gives out a shriek of laughter. 'Jason, no.' She pulls her foot away only for him to pounce on the other one. 'Jason, please,' she lets out a really loud scream of laughter. 'Oh, stop,' she gasps, 'you know I'm ticklish there.'

'Am I the biggest poseur in Cartford?'

'No, no, you're not.' Jason lets go of her foot. Lauren stares up at him. 'You're the biggest poseur in the world.' She reaches out and pulls him down on to the bed. 'The biggest poseur in the world,' she whispers in his ear. Then he starts to kiss her, almost smothering her with kisses as his body presses closer and closer to hers. And it's as if she's being swept away on a giant wave, carrying her further and further away from Grant, from everything, until all she can feel is this strange ache inside her which makes her tremble with happiness.

'I'M JUST GOING TO SEE IF I LEFT MY BOOK IN THE BEDROOM.'

The wave crashes to earth as they both spring up. The great roar of a voice is still vibrating around her room. Then, she hears someone lumber past. 'That's my dad,' she says, 'he always does that if he thinks things are getting too passionate in here.'

Jason doesn't reply, just puts his arm around her and then kisses her lightly on the neck.

'I'M GOING TO STAY UP HERE AND SORT THROUGH A FEW THINGS IN THE OFFICE.'

'Now he's wondering why it's gone all quiet in here. Sorry.' They wrench themselves apart. 'That's okay,' says Jason. 'If I had a daughter who looked like you, I'd do just the same. I like your dad. He's a good bloke.'

'I think he likes you too – after the initial shock. You know, you're the first boy who's come in here and spoken to him as an equal. I mean, my dad rips the heads off boyfriends. And normally they come in all nervous, their lips dragging on the floor. But you weren't nervous at all, were you?'

Jason stretches out on the bed. 'I psyched myself up beforehand, that's the secret. Before a big football match I'd do that. Then you can just go charging in there.' Now he's looking into her eyes. 'By the way, what's wrong?'

'What do you mean?'

'Something's wrong. I can tell.' Lauren stares at him, quite shocked by his noticing that. She'd deliberately not told him about her encounter with Grant yesterday. Well, what was the point? He'd only get mad and rush off to Grant's house with a baseball bat and a Rottweiler.

'Was it me buying that car?' Yesterday Jason had taken Lauren to see this Beetle which he'd bought for three hundred pounds. And when Lauren saw it, well, it was a wreck that belonged on a rubbish tip. Jason kept going on about how he was going to do it up but Lauren, who was in a foul mood anyway, had been distinctively sour about it all.

'No, I'm sorry if I was a bit off yesterday but it wasn't that, honestly.'

'So there is something,' declares Jason, 'and don't try lying to me now because I am the man who knows all things.'

And suddenly, Lauren really wants to tell him,

just like she used to – 'Jason, there's this guy in the village who keeps following us,' or, 'Jason, we've got to stay late at school on Tuesday.' Now, once more, the words rush out. 'Jason, I saw Grant yesterday . . .' and he doesn't say a word, doesn't interrupt her once, but then he never does in situations like this. He'll just sit there, his eyes fastened on to you. And when she finishes he lets out a low whistle, then he gets up, and does his familiar pan-ther-like pacing around her room.

'That guy's off his face and I ought to go round his house and break his kneecaps,' he snarls.

'No,' says Lauren.

'Oh, go on,' says Jason, 'he deserves it.'

'No, I don't want you to do that,' says Lauren firmly. 'That's just immature.'

'Fun, though.'

'No, and besides, it won't help me.'

He raises his hand. 'All right then, there's only one other alternative.'

'What's that?'

'Well, if it comes to a battle between you and Grant, Grant's going to win every time.'

'You reckon?'

'Definitely. He's older, he's got status. He's got to win.'

'So I've lost, then.'

Jason doesn't appear to hear. 'Anyway, that guy, he's bad news. He's not genuine. I knew that right away. Stay in his class and you'll have more trouble.

So there's only one way out.' Lauren looks up. 'Join an English class he doesn't teach. Is there one?'

'Well, yes,' says Lauren slowly. 'There's an English group which meet on Monday morning – that's a bit of a drag – and Tuesday afternoon. It'd also mean I lose my one day off a week, but still . . .'

'You'd be out of Grant's class,' says Jason. 'He'd have nothing on you. You've wiped him out completely.'

'Yes, that's true . . . Of course, there'd be extra work starting a new group, they may not even be doing the same books.'

'But you'll handle it. You've got the talent.'

She smiles as the idea grows in her head. 'I wouldn't mind leaving that awful group anyway and making a fresh start – and people change groups all the time at college.' She stands up. 'And maybe Cathy would change with me. She hates Grant too. Oh, Jason, it's all so simple really, isn't it?'

'Best solutions usually are.'

'The only thing is, I hate to think of Grant winning.'

Jason shakes his head. 'He hasn't won, no way. He's lost what he most wanted – you.'

She stares up at him. 'And I've been so anxious, so depressed.'

He grins. 'Don't be depressed. Life's great. Now let's go and have a drink.' And before she can reply he's out of the door. On the landing they discover Lauren's dad, hovering. He pretends to be looking for something.

'We're just going out for a while, Dad,' she says.

'All right, but don't be late again, will you?' says her dad. 'Last night, Jason, you kept Lauren out past twelve o'clock. I thought, here's her new boyfriend sticking up two fingers at me, her father. Who does he think he is, royalty or something?'

'Won't happen again.' says Jason. 'Little slip-up, that's all. You have my word on that, Bill.'

'All right, Jason, all right. Well, enjoy yourselves.'

'Thanks, Dad,' says Lauren. She kisses him lightly on the cheek and whispers, 'And you can go back down and watch *Inspector Morse* now.'

They race out into a mild November evening and there are a surprising number of people out, enjoying this burst of good weather.

'The White Hart?' asks Jason.

'Wherever,' says Lauren, 'I don't care. I just feel suddenly, wonderfully, gloriously FREE.' As they stroll along Lauren spots two boys from her Communications group. They're both a good laugh and wave frantically. 'Well, hi,' says Lauren, giving them a flirty smile. They point at her mini-skirt, and howl. And Lauren calls out, 'See you tomorrow,' before they disappear into the newsagent.

'You go on,' says Jason, 'I'm going to get you some chocolate.'

'There's no need,' begins Lauren.

'It's okay, I'll catch you up,' and before she can say anything else, Jason has already charged across the road.

Inside the shop the two boys are buying cigarettes.

Jason stares levelly at them. He's trying hard to steady himself. For his head is thumping furiously. He still can't believe the way these guys leered at Lauren – and that was when Jason was there. As they go to leave the shop, Jason is suddenly standing in front of them. 'All right lads,' his voice is both friendly yet menacing. They gaze at him suspiciously. 'My name's Jason,' he says. Already the two guys are backing away, 'and that young lady you just spoke to is mine and if you go near her again, I'll break your necks – got it?' The first guy's adam's apple goes up about nine inches. The second guy mutters, 'Yeah, we got it . . . hardly know her anyway.' 'Keep it that way,' snaps Jason.

The guys bolt for the door and rush out. Jason follows behind, his head still hammering away. Then he tears up the road after Lauren.

'What chocolate did you get, then?' she asks.

'Chocolate?' Jason had forgotten all about that. 'Couldn't buy anything in there,' he says. 'Scummy shop, full of scummy people.' Then he puts his arm tightly around Lauren.

Every evening, just after dinner, Giles cleans his mouth out. It is always a disgusting spectacle but tonight, Cathy thinks, he excels himself, with his tongue really digging around in those back teeth. But it's the accompanying squelching noises that make Cathy want to heave. Finally, the tongue comes to the front of his mouth and he bites it, that's how he always ends these clean-ups. Cathy's an

61

expert on it. Surely, one day soon, her mum will turn to him and snap, 'Giles, not again. You're being gross.' Surely, one day soon, her mum will throw him out – on his tongue.

Cathy's been waiting for that joyous event for over a year now. His bluff, jovial act might fool her mum and her little sister but Cathy's had him sussed from the start; he's grumpy, selfish, ignorant, calculating and vain. Even her mum must have clocked the amount of time he spends in the bathroom. That's why Cathy used to set her alarm extra early. But as soon as she stepped out of the bathroom, there he'd be, puffing impatiently. And Cathy especially hated having to see him first thing in the morning. For that's a private time, isn't it. Sometimes he'd even bang on the door while she was in the bathroom. But when she complained to her mum, she just said, 'Oh, he doesn't mean anything by it. That's only his way.'

Yet, actually, all the time he's out to undermine Cathy. Like this evening, she'd persuaded her mum to cook a vegetarian meal and her mum was saying, 'I'm getting quite keen on these vegetarian meals and I'm sure they're better for you, too,' when he rolled into the kitchen and wailed, 'But there's no meat.' Then he said, 'I suppose this is all Cathy's doing. It's just a phase she's going through, you know.' That made Cathy furious. She nearly said to him, 'Actually, you're the phase.'

She gets up, 'I'm just going to ring Lauren.'

'Be quicker to walk round, wouldn't it?' he says, 'and cheaper.'

Cathy glares at him. 'You can bill me for the call if you like.' Then she exits. Trust him to have to stick his nose into everything. Still, she liked the way she'd said that, dignified but cutting.

She picks the phone up. Poor Lauren. All day at college she'd been so depressed about this Grant business. It sounds awful but in a way Cathy is quite looking forward to escaping into Lauren's problems.

Lauren's father answers the phone. 'Oh, hello, Mr Davies, is Lauren there please?'

'That's Cathy, isn't it,' he says warmly. Cathy is a favourite of his. 'You've just missed her I'm afraid, left about two minutes ago with Jason.' Of course, Jason. Cathy'd totally forgotten he'd be round at Lauren's this evening. 'But I'm sure you can catch them up, they went . . .'

Cathy stops listening. She can't go chasing after them like that. If they'd wanted her to come too they'd have rung her. She wonders if Lauren has told Jason about what happened with Grant yesterday. She said she wouldn't but . . . Cathy feels a sudden stab of jealousy; Cathy's the one Lauren discusses her problems with, no one else. Now she's being pathetic. It's only natural Lauren would chat with her boyfriend about, well, all sorts of things. Cathy can't mark off certain areas of Lauren as belonging to her. And instead of standing here being silly, she should ring someone else. How about Becky? Why not ask her out for a drink? Good idea.

63

No, hold on, isn't Becky meeting Adam later on tonight? Well, so what, she can still meet Cathy for a drink first. But what if Becky doesn't want to go out? Might she feel she has to say 'Yes' to Cathy so as not to hurt her feelings? And Cathy has an absolute horror of people doing that. Sometimes even ringing people up is a huge effort. Cathy always fears the person she's ringing is doing something absolutely fascinating – and the last thing they want is to be pulled away to talk to her. That's how she feels now.

She's just being feeble, isn't she? But then she suspects that basically, she's quite a feeble person. People are always calling her a "nice girl" but then, what is nice: someone who doesn't upset people. Why – because they're feeble.

Now, if only Jez were here she'd definitely have rung him. But he's not and he hasn't answered her last two letters . . . She can feel a nasty depression just waiting to settle over her. No, she won't let it.

She goes upstairs to her bedroom and decides to copy up the Communications notes. She sits at her desk and puts some mushy tapes (how Adam would hate them) on her ghetto-blaster. She switches the tape up – music distracts her if it's on too low – and starts working. It's not very exciting but it is oddly soothing, and she can feel herself relaxing in a boring but steady rhythm, when suddenly her bedroom door swings open and Giles bursts in, lurching straight over to her desk. At first, thinking he must be drunk or something Cathy shrinks away in horror. But then she sees him move the switch on her

64

ghetto-blaster. He turns the music right down, then yells, 'Can't hear ourselves think down there,' and without another word gusts out again.

Cathy is too stunned to say anything at first. She still can't believe he did that. The nerve of him, lunging into her room like that without even knocking. How dare he! Well, he's not getting away with that. Cathy immediately switches her ghetto-blaster up as far as it will go and sits and waits . . . This time she will be ready for him. But it is lighter footsteps she hears this time.

Her mum knocks, then stands in the doorway. 'Cathy, love, can you switch it down a bit, we're trying to watch a television programme.'

'I will because you asked me,' said Cathy, but even as she says that she notices how childish she sounds. And it's vital her mum appreciates how badly Giles behaved. 'He just tore into my room, you know, didn't even have the courtesy to knock, then without asking, switched my music down.' Come on, Mum, she thinks, get outraged, please. But her mum just nods mildly. 'We couldn't hear the television at all, you see.'

'But he just burst into my room, Mum.' She can hear her voice rising. 'That's not right, is it?' Her mum looks pale and anxious and tired. Her tone is conciliatory. 'He's had quite a hard day at work and he was looking forward to . . .' But Cathy doesn't want to hear any of this. She wants her mum to say, 'Yes, Giles was out of order. He shouldn't have done that.' Instead, all she gets are tense smiles and feeble excuses.

'I'm putting a lock on my door first thing in the morning,' she cries, desperately. Her mum doesn't even seem to hear. 'I know how annoying it is having to keep your music down . . .' She's being so polite, much more polite in fact than she would have been when Dad was alive. Then she would have just said, 'Switch your music down please, Cathy.' Cathy would much rather she spoke to her in that way now. For this new politeness is oddly chilling; it's the way you might address a guest. Suddenly, Cathy's a guest in her own home. Next they'll be asking her to hand her keys in every time she goes out.

Mum peers at the homework. 'So how's it coming on?'

'Fine.'

'When you're finished, come down and join us.' US!

'Mum, I wish you could have seen the way he came in here.' One last attempt.

'I think we're all a bit tired, aren't we?' says her mum. 'It's been one of those days . . . if we can all make allowances . . . See you later.'

Cathy switches the music off, draws the curtains and lies on her bed. And there it comes again and this time she can't hold it back. The depression descends over her like a huge fog. And it starts devouring her right away, pushing her down, deeper and deeper.

Her life's awful, isn't it? She even lost her job at

the Record Room today – well, the place is closing down. She liked working there, too and she won't get another job as good. And she must get another job to pay for her driving lessons which she's crap at . . . of course. She's crap at everything. Life is crap.

She sighs. This depression is settling in for the night, isn't it? Maybe this one will never lift. Perhaps she'll end up like those girls who are permanently miserable or those boys who say everything's "boring". Still, it'd make a change from a Cathy who smiles too much and is always trying to help people. Yet, at the end of all that smiling and helping she's quite alone. No one really needs her. Not even Lauren now. No one, except for the animals. They need her and she is helping them. Maybe even saving a few lives. Her animal rights is the only important thing she's ever done. If it weren't for that . . .

She coughs. She can even taste the fog now. Down below she hears them all laughing away at some brain-dead comedy, her sister too, little traitor. She clutches her arms around herself and gazes upwards at the ceiling. Yes, there they are, all the stars her dad put up there for her, years ago now. He said, 'Now you've got your own private little galaxy.' And then he started telling her how all the stars in the sky which look so close together are actually light years apart from each other. How her dad loved telling her little facts like that. Every time they went for a walk he'd say, 'Now this tree is called . . . And that plant over there, that's a . . .' And the stars are light years apart. That's how she feels, far, far away from everyone, stranded on her own little planet, which is just a wilderness, anyway.

Up comes the rumble of laughter again. And his louder than anyone else. Is there nowhere she can escape from him? Oh, Dad, why did you have to go? Why couldn't you have waited, at least until I was eighteen, like all normal fathers? And now look who's taken your place. You'd hate him, Dad. He's nothing like you. And tonight he charged into my room like a wild animal. But no one else sees what I see. No one understands. So I'm left just drifting . . . light years apart from everyone.

'Becky, look,' cries Adam. He points across the lake to a pinky light which is edging its way across the pitch-dark sky.

'How weird,' she exclaims. 'It's getting light over there but not here. It's like when it's raining on one side of the house but not on the other, isn't it? When I was a little girl that used to send me mad.'

It was, what Adam termed, a mellow night, so they had left the hut early and gone for a walk. They ended up walking four-and-a-half miles so that they could sit by the lake. There wasn't even the hint of another person about, just a wonderful stillness, as they snuggled together, watching the sky across the lake fill up with colour.

'You know,' says Becky, 'my cousin's always going on about these May Balls she went to at university and most of it sounds pretty kiddish, like having food fights . . .'

'Food fights can be good fun,' murmurs Adam.

'Well, yes,' concedes Becky. 'But anyway, the only bit I really envied her was when she said how she and her boyfriend took a bottle of champagne and sat by the lake and watched the dawn come up. I really fancied that and now I'm doing it.'

'Apart from the champagne. Next time . . .'

She laughs, then says, 'It is a beautiful sight, isn't it? You just don't think of this happening every night. It makes you feel . . . oh, I don't know, as if everything's much more mysterious and important than we ever think.'

' "No eternal reward shall forgive us for wasting the dawn." Jim Morrison.' Adam half-laughs. 'He was always saying crazy things like that.'

'No, I like that. Have you ever written poetry?'

'Never. Not when I was supposed to. But then I did this computer course, all about information technology or something and we were supposed to re-arrange these charts, only I soon got sick of doing that and I started writing all these poems, until the guy who was in charge of the course caught me and he went mad. He goes, "If you write one more poem you're out of the course." '

'And what did you do?'

'I wrote another poem, this really sarcastic one about how if I was chucked off this course my life would be over. And I got thrown out.'

'I'd love to read some of your poetry.'

'I don't know if I've kept any.'

'I bet you have. Please.'

'Yeah, well maybe. I'll have to read it again first. It might all be rubbish now.'

'At school, were you a bit of a rebel?'

He considers this. 'I don't know what I was, really.'

'That's what Mark said. He was telling me how at school you had different groups, like the lads and the drop-outs, and so on, and you didn't fit into any of them.'

'I suppose I was a drop-out in a way. Like my hair was really long and "hey man" and I remember one afternoon, Mark and me coming back to school drunk. And Mark got caught right away, suspended for two days, it was quite a big deal, and yet no one noticed I was drunk as well. I just sat hunched in a corner and no one bothered me.' He grins, 'I guess they thought I was permanently spaced-out anyway. I know my parents did.'

'They haven't said anything, have they, about . . . ?'

'No, but – well I can't explain it really. I just get this feeling that they're watching me and wondering . . . It's as if they've got these time-bombs in their heads . . .'

'Just waiting to explode,' Becky shudders.

'Forget 'em,' says Adam. 'They've got nothing to do with this, this is our time.'

The lake is flooded with colour now. But the sky above them remains obstinately black.

'Let's not go back,' says Becky, 'until all this sky is just blazing with light.'

'I've got a better idea,' says Adam. 'Let's not go back at all. One day we won't, you know. One day we'll just disappear.'

It is after six o'clock when Adam finally walks Becky home. 'There's the milkman,' Becky giggles. 'He'll be wondering where I've been. Not that I care.' She yawns. 'It's funny, isn't it, all the time I've been with you I haven't felt tired at all but now, here . . .' she yawns again.

'It must be love,' whispers Adam. He watches Becky walk up her drive, turn the key twice in her lock and blow him a huge kiss, before disappearing. Tonight, Adam is so tempted to rush after her. Instead he stands there, his eyes smarting. Then finally he begins the trudge home. By the time he reaches his house his eyelids are feeling heavy, in fact his whole body feels heavy. He clambers wearily on to the porch. Then, as he climbs through his bed-room window, he hears something crash out of his back pocket and on to the porch.

He freezes. Then he stares below at the loose change. Why the hell did he put money in his jeans? Now he's got his parents up – or has he? He can't hear anything. Finally, he creeps inside his bed-room, oozing relief. He hasn't a clue how that change got into his back-pocket. Surely he wouldn't have put it there? But he must have. Who else would put money in his jeans? He shakes his head. He's just so absent-minded sometimes (all the time).

71

He quickly whips into bed. What's the time – a quarter-to-seven. Hardly worth going to sleep. He'll be woken up again at half-seven. Then he's got to catch up on all the work he's missed at college. He's really falling behind. Still, worry about that later . . . for now, he'll just think about Becky.

But he's barely closed his eyes when his door bangs open and he hears his father calling his name. Adam keeps his eyes shut. Just pretend to be asleep, but his heart's thumping insanely. What can have happened?

Now his father's calling his name again and then he pulls all the covers off his bed. Adam squints round. He can hardly speak.

'Dad' he gasps, 'what's happened?'

'You can stop pretending,' snarls his father. 'And I want you downstairs, NOW.'

4 *Discovery*

Adam jumps up. He's only wearing his underpants so he scrambles into his jeans and for some reason, his brown leather jacket, and stumbles downstairs.

They are waiting for him in the kitchen. Mum seated at the large wooden table in her quilted dressing gown, her eyes huge, her face deathly pale. Dad dressed in his white shirt and beige trousers, staring out of the window. Often when there's a thunderstorm his dad will come downstairs, make a huge pot of tea and stand watching what he calls, 'the entertainment'. Tonight though, his dad's hands are clenched tightly behind his back and he looks as if he's struggling to control himself. When he finally turns round his face is bright red. 'You,' he begins. But anger chokes back all the other words. Instead, he dives forward and grabs Adam by his jacket. 'You . . . you . . . do you know we nearly called the police? Have you any idea of all the worry you have caused us? Have you?' His dad's in full flow now.

'I'm sorry,' gulps Adam.

'We know exactly what's been going on,' rages his father. 'Don't even try lying to us. So I want *you* to tell us the truth.' His father relaxes his hold on Adam's jacket and Adam drops on to a chair. But his father is still glowering over him. He'll be waving flashlights into Adam's face next. And his mum is up and circling round too.

'I went out to meet someone,' says Adam.

'Who?' demand his parents, in stereo.

Adam hesitates. When he was younger he kept having this dream, in which he was being chased by these shadowy but menacing figures and he always ended up on top of this cliff, thousands of feet high. He could hear them gaining on him, so his only way out was to jump. He'd stand right on the edge and then suddenly, he'd close his eyes and leap off and hope that somehow he'd land in the sea. Adam closes his eyes. 'A girl,' he says.

'And what did you and this girl do?' asks his father. We made mad passionate love for five hours – that's what Adam wants to say, for his father's 'tell me the worst' tone of voice really narks him.

'We sat by the lake and watched the dawn come up,' he says, as flatly as he can. No one speaks for a moment, then his dad releases a tiny smile and his mum lets out a low sigh of relief. And far away in his head he hears a splash; the sound of someone landing in the sea.

His dad pulls up a chair, his face now a healthier pink colour, saying, 'You had us thinking all sorts,' while his mum grumbles, 'I don't know why you couldn't have seen this girl in the day. Do we know her? Who is she?' Should he make a name up? No, it'll only create more muddles in the end. Besides, why should he have to lie?

'Actually, it's Becky.' Voice casual, but strong.

'Mark's girlfriend,' says his mum at once.

'She's not Mark's girlfriend any more,' says Adam.

'Ah well, I thought,' begins his mum. 'No, I'm not surprised . . . but why do you have to hide her away from your family? Why can't you bring her round? Aren't we always hospitable to your friends?'

'It is good,' adds his dad unexpectedly, 'that you're interested in girls again.' Adam stares at him impatiently. He's not talking about 'girls'. He's talking about one girl. His girl. Becky.

'You must promise us,' says his dad, 'that you will never sneak out at night again like this.'

'Apart from anything else, it is very dangerous,' says his mum. 'Oh, what a night you've given us.'

'I'm sorry,' says Adam, feeling a quick spurt of guilt for them. 'You heard me leave, then?'

His mum nods. 'When I heard you, I was certain we were being burgled.'

'She pushed me down into the garden,' says his dad, 'telling me there's someone out there. Then your mother happened to look in on you,' he smiles, 'had me driving all round Cartford, while you were romancing your female admirer.'

Adam thinks with a shudder how awful it would

75

have been if his dad had seen him and Becky walking along together. In his mind he can see his dad's car screeching to a stop right beside them and Adam thinking, no, it can't be, how is it possible? And Becky, poor Becky, shaking beside him.

Then he hears his mum saying, 'I know some very nice girls, just about your age . . .' but his dad gives her a warning glance as if to say, 'Not now.' Then he gets up, rubbing his hands together. 'Well, it's just gone seven o'clock, so if we're lucky we might get half-an-hour's sleep before the alarm goes . . .' They tumble upstairs. Adam's eyes are flaming with tiredness but even before he lies down he knows he won't sleep.

Too many images keep flashing through his head. Images of Becky and him tonight and then, like an accompanying soundtrack, that's the last time you'll be able to meet like this. But it'll be better now, won't it? He can see Becky freely, even bring her home to tea. And his parents will be so nice – to her face. Yet, behind their smiles of welcome they'll be praying that next time, Adam will bring a different girl home to them. For they won't worry if they think Adam's – as his father would say – 'playing the field,' before he meets that nice Jewish girl. Then, and only then, will he be allowed to be serious. Adam punches his pillow with frustration. And he thought he'd landed in the water – only he's underwater, plunging to the bottom. But he won't let them push him down.

He sits up, gasping for air. He feels as if he's being smothered and his throat's just so dry . . . He's tiptoeing along to the bathroom when he notices a light under his parents' door. There's whispering too. He's about to walk on when he hears his name. He immediately stops and listens.

His mum is saying, 'No, we can't blame him, what else can we expect, there's no real Jewish centre here, no sense of commitment.' Then her voice fades out, until the end of her next sentence . . . 'got to move away.' Then he hears his dad's rumble. 'No, we can't move away.' Adam breathes again. 'There's no point anyway, he'll be at university before we know it.' He says something about Reuben too. Adam can't make out all of it but he can guess; Reuben's grown up in the same area and he's never caused any problems.

But his mum comes back, hardly whispering at all now, 'Reuben's very special. No, we are completely to blame for this. We have failed our son and now Adam needs guiding.' What does that mean?

His dad murmurs something Adam can't hear but it was probably, 'Keep your voice down,' for their voices are so low now that even when Adam presses his ear right up to the door he can't make out what else they're plotting.

But he's heard enough. And forgetting all about the glass of water, he sneaks back to his room. No point in trying to sleep now. Whenever he closes his eyes, three words keep springing out at him. 'ADAM NEEDS GUIDING'.

*

'You're late,' cries Becky as her mum thumps her shopping down on the kitchen table.

'Yes, well I got held up,' replies her mum. She walks into the lounge, where Becky is having tea and toast before leaving for her evening shift at *Pizza Paradiso*.

'I went into the bookshop to display all the copies of my books when Mrs Rosen caught me.' Becky stops chewing. 'She told me, it's Adam you're seeing, not Mark.'

'I was going to tell you.'

'And that you've been seeing Adam for some time now.'

'Yes, we had to keep it secret, Mum, so Adam's parents wouldn't find out.

Her mum doesn't reply, just rolls her eyes. Then she goes back into the kitchen again. Becky follows her. Her mum switches on the kettle and starts noisily putting tins away while Becky hovers in the doorway.

'I didn't tell you, Mum, because I thought it would put you in a difficult position with Mrs Rosen. I know you have a real thing about honesty.'

'I certainly hate being lied to,' says her mum, hurling the tins into the cupboard, 'lies always make me feel slightly mad. Perhaps because they make you doubt everything.'

Becky edges forward, 'I'm sorry,' she whispers.

'Of course, I don't know why we feel we should know what's going on in the heart and soul of our children.' The kettle switches itself off. 'Coffee?'

'No, I don't want any coffee,' cries Becky. 'I want you to listen to me. I hated lying to you – and stop doing that.'

'What?'

'Rolling your eyes at me all the time. That is just so annoying.' Becky is shaking with both guilt and anger now. 'I didn't want to lie to you. But I couldn't risk losing him, that's why I did it.'

Her mum stops unpacking the shopping and draws up a chair. 'I'm making too much of this. I certainly lied to your nan. She always said to me, "Can you look me in the face and say that," and if I could she believed me. She didn't know that I could lie my head off and still look right into her eyes.' She smiles. 'Still, I thought when I'm a mum, I shall be so wonderful that my daughter will tell me everything, always.'

'Mum, I am . . .'

'No, don't apologise again. Perhaps keeping secrets from our parents is something we have to go through, a stage in our movement towards autonomy or something.'

'Mum, what I wanted to . . .'

'And having your parents know everything about you must be terribly claustrophobic.'

'Mum, will you stop talking when I'm trying to interrupt.'

'Go on, then.'

'I was just going to ask what Mrs Rosen said about Adam and me.'

Her mum gets up, pours both Becky and herself a

mug of coffee, then replies, 'Mrs Rosen said how nice it was that you and Adam were friends.'

'Oh.'

'The sub-text of our scene together I interpreted as "and make sure that they stay as just friends".'

'Too late, we're way, way beyond that,' says Becky flatly.

'I guessed that. And I'm sure Mrs Rosen has as well, really. Still, it's not going to be easy, you know. In fact it could become rather nasty.'

'But he's the one, Mum. I know it – I know it in my every corpuscle. And no one will ever break us up.'

Her mum laughs, but not unkindly. 'Well, I'd better have this paragon round for dinner soon, hadn't I?'

Adam watches him walk in. He's wearing large horn-rimmed glasses and a blue suit which he hasn't quite grown into. He stares around the garage shop and curls his lip a bit. His whole manner suggests someone who's slumming.

He picks up a pound box of chocolates and some sweets, and spins them across the counter. Then he waves a twenty pound note at Adam. 'I hope you can change this.' He's got one of those really annoying voices too; the kind which are always smirking at you.

Each customer tonight has been addressed by Adam in a different accent – well, it passes the time. For the last customer, Adam had adopted a hearty

Scottish accent. But for this one Adam decides on a creepily polite voice.

'Well, I'll see if we can help you, sir. Ah yes, sir, we can, there's your change, sir.'

The guy stands in front of Adam, checking his change. Then he picks up one of the wine glasses from the Christmas promotion: THIS WEEK ONLY: BUY FIVE POUNDS' WORTH OF PETROL AND GET A WINE GLASS *FREE*.

'And I'll take this for my trouble too.'

Any other customer could have taken ten wine glasses and Adam wouldn't have cared – ugly, chunky things they are anyway – but not this one.

'I'm very sorry, sir,' says Adam, 'but you can only take away one of those delightful wine glasses if you've purchased five pounds' worth of petrol.'

'But that's outrageous. I have spent the equivalent amount of money here.'

'Yes, I believe that is true. But if you check the notice, I think you will see it states that the wine glasses are free only with petrol. I don't believe it says anything about chocolates. Would you like to just check it, sir?'

"Sir" gives him a look, before spluttering, 'I have never heard such nonsense. I demand you give me one of those glasses.'

The shop door opens and even before he looks up, Adam somehow knows that it is Becky. He gives her a large smile, then says, 'I'm sorry, sir, but I cannot let you take away one of our wine glasses.' His voice remains polite and calm but inside, he's just so juiced up.

'How old are you?' demands the man.

'I'm seventeen, sir.'

'Well, you're clearly far too young to be left alone in charge like this.'

Adam can feel Becky bristling. 'I won't ask how old you are, sir, because that's bad manners, but at the moment you're behaving just like my little cousin, sir – he's seven.' Becky stifles a giggle while the guy's chin wobbles furiously.

'I'm reporting you,' he says, suddenly brandishing a notebook. 'Come on, what's your name?'

'My name, sir, is Jim Morrison.'

The guy solemnly writes the name down. Adam winks at Becky who has her hand over her mouth now. The guy sweeps to the door, then gives a sly smile. 'May as well fill up with petrol, too. I'll be back to collect my glass.'

As soon as he leaves, Becky cries, 'You were brilliant, Adam, the way you kept your voice so serious . . . what are you doing?' For Adam is sitting by the petrol pump controls.

'That toe-rag hasn't won yet,' he says. 'Go and watch him out of the window, Becky. Tell me what he's doing.'

'He's just filling his car up . . . hold on, the pump's stopped.' She turns to Adam. 'What's happened?'

'I put a lock on it, keep watching.'

'Now he's examining it in a very puzzled way. Now

he's . . . Oh no, you switched the petrol on again, didn't you?' Adam nods, smiling grimly. 'And it's shot out all over his hands, his suit. Oh, Adam, look!'

But there isn't any time for Adam to look, because the guy is already storming into the shop again, dripping petrol everywhere. 'You did that, didn't you?'

Adam stands up. 'I'm afraid I did, yes, sir.'

'Well, I'm sending you the bill for this – and I'm reporting you. Oh yes, I'll have you, Morrison,' and he's so angry he nearly walks into the door.

'Well, what a shame,' says Adam. 'He forgot to collect his glass.'

'And he never paid for his petrol,' says Becky.

Adam sits back in his chair. 'I can't believe I did that.'

'Neither can I,' says Becky.

He shakes his head. 'When I started here, I thought, here I am in the outside world and I was going to be so sensible, so mature. And look at me. It was like that guy and me were fighting a duel and I just had to win. Do you think I'm going crazy?'

'No,' she pauses, 'I think you always were crazy.' She gives one of her teasing smiles. 'And will Mr Morrison lose his job?'

'Yeah, and Mr Rosen. But I'll get another one,' he grins. 'Maybe at the *Pizza Paradiso*.'

'Yes, well I put a word in for Cathy and she starts there next week but, somehow, I can't picture you there.'

'Oh, I'm very versatile and I'll definitely get something,' says Adam. 'Got to keep our fighting fund going.'

Last week Adam and Becky had decided to put their earnings together, so then they'd have money – well, they weren't quite sure what the money was for, really. Adam had said 'emergencies' and they'd left it at that.

Adam asks, 'By the way, your mum didn't mind me ringing you last night, did she? I know it was after midnight.'

'No, not at all.'

'I just thought she sounded a bit off.'

'No.'

'You know I kept waking up last night and thinking I could be sitting by the lake with Becky now, watching the dawn come up.'

'Last night, we'd have frozen,' smiles Becky.

'No, we wouldn't. You could have borrowed one of my thermal vests.'

'Oh, lovely,' she says, sliding on to his lap.

A customer comes in and Adam serves him, with Becky still sitting on his lap. Then he says, 'Just for a change, had a bit of a row with my mum last night.'

'What was it about, as if I can't guess?' Becky can feel herself stiffening already.

'Oh, she arranged for this girl from the local Jewish Social Club to ring me up and give me a real sales pitch. She went on for ages about what a jolly time they have, practically begged me to come along, no membership fees the first week . . .'

'And are you going?' asks Becky softly.

'No way. I hate anything organised like that. So then I tell my mum she was well out of order arranging that behind my back. And she says, I just thought you might like it, now you're going out more again.'

Becky can feel herself tightening with anger. She'll try anything to get Adam away from me, won't she? Only last week Becky had gone round to Adam's house for tea and been quite revoltingly sweet to his parents, desperate to win them round. And they'd all smiled and talked together about so many boring subjects until Becky wanted to scream. Why can't they stop pretending, all this fake friendliness. They want Becky out of Adam's life, don't they?

They can't see how much Adam needs her. But Becky can and sometimes it scares her. To think she suddenly has so much importance in someone's life. It's never really happened to Becky before. Everyone else Becky knows could carry on quite happily without her, except, perhaps, Mark and her mum. No, her mum would be okay. She'd still have her writing. But if she left Adam, well, he'd fall apart – and that's not being big-headed. For, you see, he's got nothing else. Just Becky. She's his life, now.

'Mark came round earlier.'

'Oh yeah.'

'Just stayed for a few minutes. Came round last night as well. It was good to see him.' Ever since Adam's parents found out about Adam and Becky, Mark's been surprisingly sympathetic. And he lets Becky rattle on about things for hours, in fact he's the one person she can talk to about this. Her mum's been good too.

The shop door opens again. 'Adam.' Adam immediately gets up, and walking towards them is a plumpish boy with a very large face, which is both friendly, yet oddly unformed. Becky instantly recognises him from the barmitzvah photograph at Adam's house. It's Reuben, Adam's older brother, wearing a tweed jacket and flannel trousers.

'Hey, Reuben,' cries Adam, 'this is a surprise.' Then Adam says, 'And Reuben, this is Becky – my girlfriend.' He says it really proudly too. They shake hands, then there is a slightly embarrassing silence after which Becky says, 'Well, I'd better go, I'm due at the *Pizza Paradiso*.'

'Ah, that must be interesting,' says Reuben.

Becky smiles. 'Not really.'

'Before you go, Becky,' says Adam. He bends down under the counter and produces a red rose in cellophane, which he drops into a glass. Yet, even as he's giving Becky the rose, he's thinking, that rose will be dead in a few days. That's why he nearly bought her a silk rose. But when he asked Cathy about this, she said, 'Oh no, you can't get her an artificial rose, that's tacky.' Adam can't see how giving your girlfriend something everlasting is tacky, but he stayed with the real rose, just to be on the safe side.

Becky sniffs it. She looks really chuffed.

'And look after the glass, won't you?' says Adam.

'I will treasure it,' says Becky. 'As it's not every customer who gets one of these.' She grins.

86

Then they turn round to Reuben, who is watching them with a faint smile on his lips.

'I'll ring you later,' says Adam. Becky kisses him lightly on the lips.

'Very nice to have met you,' says Reuben politely.

'And you,' calls Becky.

After she's gone, Reuben says, 'She's certainly attractive.'

'And hasn't she got the most amazing eyes you've ever seen?' Adam stops himself and smiles. 'So, anyway, what are you doing here? It's not the end of term already, is it?'

'That's right. Four weeks holiday now.'

'I suppose you passed all your exams?'

Reuben just smiles faintly again, then says, 'Got home this afternoon.' The rise in his voice seems to be asking, 'And where were you?'

'I haven't been home yet – it's easier to go straight on to work from college.'

'Sure.'

'What have they been saying about me, then?'

'Nothing really . . . it's just . . .'

'Yeah. Come on. Tell me.'

Reuben looks embarrassed. 'They got a letter from the college.'

Adam freezes. 'Did they . . .' Suddenly he can't talk in sentences. 'Am I . . .' He takes a breath. 'My death warrant, was it?'

'No, no.' Reuben tousles his hair. 'It was just a little warning, that's all. It said you've been missing lessons, not doing any homework.'

'Too right, I haven't. But still . . .' Adam sinks back into his chair. 'Never thought they'd do it. I know I'm a bit behind with my work. I bet Mum and Dad went ape, didn't they?'

Reuben hesitates. 'They're worried about you.'

'I worry about myself sometimes.' He looks up at Reuben, 'I know I should be working. And I want to work – but still I don't. I mean, I go to the library, get all the books out and just sit there staring into space. When I was younger I could work all right, couldn't I?' Reuben nods. 'But now, I just can't make myself care enough about it. How do you keep working, Reuben? Come on, tell me the secret.'

Reuben laughs. 'There's no secret. It just has to be done if you want to get anywhere.'

'But some days doesn't it all just seem really unimportant?' Adam gets up. 'At university, have you got any girlfriends?'

'Oh yes,' says Reuben. 'Everyone's quite friendly.'

'No, I mean, is there anyone special?'

Reuben hesitates. 'I want to get all my exams first before . . . well, then I'll have something to offer a lady.'

'But she could be gone by then, Reuben.'

Reuben doesn't answer this. 'I'd better go back. Don't worry, Adam, it will all work out . . . saw the motorbike, by the way. You go out a lot on it, then?'

'Yeah, it's really zen-like, you know. I can go out and escape from . . . everything.'

'That must be a good feeling,' says Reuben. Then

he tousles his brother's hair again. 'You're not still growing, are you?'

Adam is now half a head taller than Reuben. 'I hope not.'

Reuben laughs. 'See you at home, then.' He goes to leave.

'Reuben, what have they said to you about Becky?'

'Nothing much. Only that they like her.'

'They're trying to split us up, you know.'

Reuben considers this. 'No, they wouldn't do that. They just want you and Becky to take things nice and slow. I'll see you later.'

Adam calls after him. 'You are on my side, aren't you?'

Reuben turns round and smiles. 'I've always been on your side.'

'Now, are you sure you won't come with us?' asks Cathy's mum. 'It would be lovely for us all to go out together on Christmas Eve.'

'No, I'm fine at home,' says Cathy. Then she just has to add, 'He's only taking you out for a pub lunch, you know.' For Giles has been making such a big deal out of this lunch, going on and on about it. It's like, be grateful for the rest of your life that I'm taking you out. Certainly, there's no way that Cathy would go with them.

'Well, I won't force you. It's a shame, though.' She gives Cathy a sad smile. Cathy just frowns in return. Her mum is all dressed up, with her new dangly earrings (an early Christmas present from

Giles) gleaming away. Giles pumps the horn impatiently and her mum jumps, as always. Earlier, Giles had wondered if his shirt needed 'a little iron' and her mum just sprang down the stairs with it. And when Cathy pointed out that Giles was actually perfectly capable of ironing his own shirt, her mum wittered on about 'how she enjoys doing it', which is total rubbish. How can you enjoy ironing shirts?

Cathy sighs. What does her mum see in him, she asks herself for the hundredth time. It must be sex, she decides. Most things come down to that, don't they? For in the end, what are we but mammals with a unique gift for fooling ourselves.

Cathy slams the door shut. Then she sees Scampi has sneaked into the lounge again and is sniffing away at the Christmas presents under the tree. Ah well, Cathy thinks, why should he have to wait until tomorrow. So she picks up his present and throws it on to the carpet. He dives on to it, tearing it open while manically wagging his tail. Scampi is just discovering that he's got a squeaky hamburger for Christmas, when the phone rings.

Cathy picks up the phone and at first can't hear who it is, Scampi's making so much noise. 'Scampi, no!' she cries, then returns to the phone. 'I'm sorry, who is that?'

'It's me, face-ache.'

'Jez, I don't believe it,' she exclaims, both excited and shy at the same time. 'Where are you and why haven't you written? You were supposed to be coming home for Christmas.'

'Yeah, I didn't make it.'

'I know that. Why?'

'Unsound time, Christmas, can't get served in any of the pubs; your kitchen is full of relations you hate, all standing about talking about themselves – it's not such a good time for trees either.'

'Oh, Jez, you've totally caught me by surprise. Where are you ringing from?'

'Munich, doing a few hours at a hotel here. And there's no bosses about, so I thought I'd see if you were in and getting ready for Father Christmas . . . Thanks for your card by the way. Very tasteful.'

'Thank you so much for yours,' says Cathy with undisguised sarcasm.

'Yeah, I'm sending Easter cards instead and here's a sorry in advance for not answering your letters. I did enjoy reading them, though. And I loved the photo. So, tell me the latest.'

'I wrote you that Lauren and I have gone into another English group, didn't I?'

'Yeah.'

'Well, Lauren re-wrote the essay Grant gave her an E for – and she got a B.'

'That guy really is a twat, isn't he?'

'We don't see him now but Mark and Becky reckon he's cracking up, he keeps having a go at people for no reason . . .'

'Are Jason and Lauren . . . ?'

'Still going strong. And so are Adam and Becky, despite Adam's family. And Adam's been on report at college which he wasn't too happy about. What else? Well, I've joined Becky at the *Pizza Paradiso*. We're both working a seven-hour shift on New Year's Eve, would you believe. And Adam's at the video shop now.'

'What about young Mark – has he cut his first disc yet?'

'Actually, he's doing really well, most nights he's singing somewhere now. And The White Hart is opening a special club for under-eighteens' starting on New Year's Day – and they want Mark to be the official greeter. Oh, yes, don't laugh, but I've put in for my driving test on March 29th, two weeks after Jason. My instructor still says, "I'm letting the car drive me rather than me drive the car." But Jez, there's so much to do, you've got to steer, look in the mirror and change gear all at the same time. Anyway, what about you? What are you doing?'

'I read a lot, well, until my finger gets tired. And I drink the occasional pint . . . nothing else really.'

'You must be doing something.'

'I'm working on a project called great lavatories of the world, it's just on paper at the moment.'

'Oh, ha, ha. No, come on, you still doing your waitering job in Berlin, are you?'

'From time to time. I've done a few jobs to increase the old cash flow. But I've decided, what I'm best at is doing nothing. The great thing about being here is that I can just observe things and not have to be a part of them.'

'That doesn't sound very friendly.'

'You know what I mean, though. As soon as I

come home I'll get a job as a trainee bank manager or something and get sucked into it all. And soon I'll be queueing up with my dad in the DIY centre on Saturday afternoons for our screws,' Cathy starts to laugh, 'and inviting the neighbours round to see the new knob I put on the cupboard and every weekend I'll have a drill in my hand . . .'

'Oh Jez, you won't!'

'Yeah, I will, I'll end up just like my dad and fifteen million other men. You get conditioned into it in the end. I bet if you rang my dad now he'd be out in his garage measuring up shelves. When I was younger I used to watch him and think there must be better ways of spending your time.' He pauses, then says, 'By the way, there's another reason I phoned. It's, if you don't hear from me for a bit, don't panic. But I thought I might be a real student and bum round Europe for a bit. You know, take a look at France first, then . . .'

'But Jez, that'll mean you'll be away for ages yet.'

'Well, you never know. I'm not definitely doing it. By the way, are you going out with anyone?'

'No, why?'

'I just wondered. Thought someone would have snapped you up.'

'No, no. I did have an offer last week from this guy called Graham. He went to our school actually – very tall and thin with ginger hair – he's a year younger than me.'

'Your toy-boy, then.'

'No, somehow I can't see Graham as a toy-boy.

He's a bit clumsy and unsure of himself . . . lacks confidence.'

'You could always adopt him.'

Cathy laughs, then wants to ask Jez if he's seeing anyone. But she can't bring herself to – just in case he says, 'Yes, I am.'

'I bet you're sorry you turned me down for that meal,' says Jez.

'You're never going to let me forget that, are you?'

'No, even when you're ninety I'll come and haunt you as a ghost and whisper in your ear, "You turned me down . . ." '

'Jez! You will come back eventually though, won't you?'

'Definitely.'

'You've got a sweet shop to open, remember.'

'Oh yeah, my sweet shop,' he chuckles softly. 'Me in a brown coat measuring out the dolly mixtures.'

'What are you wearing now?' asks Cathy. 'Let me guess, one of your black, baggy jumpers, all ripped.'

'That's it, hundreds of rips,' says Jez. 'Talking to you almost makes me feel homesick.'

'Aaah.'

'So are you all going out tonight?'

'Yeah, we're clubbing it. We'll start . . .'

'Hold up, Cathy, I think someone's coming. So look, have a cracking Christmas. Say hello to them all for me, and . . .'

'Jez, remember you owe me a letter. Wherever you are, you can still write . . .' but the line's gone dead. And even with Scampi squeaking away at his toy, the room seems deathly quiet.

'Mark, a question for New Year's Day. What have you done to help me today?'

'I'll have to pass on that one, Mum.'

'And what did you do to help me yesterday, or the day before?'

Mark turns round from the full-length mirror in the lounge. 'Pass again, I'm afraid.'

'So you've done nothing for the good of the family this holiday.'

'Oh, stressful.'

'And there are so many little jobs that need doing, Mark, in the garden.'

'What's a garden?'

'You might well ask. Twice I've asked you to compost all the leaves.'

'Tomorrow, Mum. I promise. I'll tell you what, if I don't compost the leaves tomorrow, may I be struck down dead.'

'Now you're being silly.'

'But tonight, Mum, is well crucial.' He turns back to the mirror. Yes, the suit is sharp. Jason helped him pick well. He pictures himself leaning forward and saying, 'Hello, pleased to welcome you to The White Hart's new under-eighteen club.'

'If you can tear yourself away from that mirror you can take your dad's tea up for him,' calls his mum from the kitchen.

Mark follows her. 'Dad still feeling a bit rough, is

95

he?' Mum shakes her head grimly. Mark goes on, 'I'm just so glad none of my friends saw Dad doing his party trick last night. At his age, too.'

'He was talked into it by people who should have known better and he'd had a little too much to drink.'

'A little! Mum, he was pi . . .'

'Thank you, Mark. He's certainly paying for it now, isn't he?' She bustles about putting a mug of tea and a plateful of biscuits on to the tray. 'And don't you go throwing your money about tonight, Mark,' she says suddenly. 'You can't buy friends.'

'I know.'

'And I know you, wanting to be in with everyone.' Mark starts edging away. 'They'll take your money and then forget all about you. No, you hang on to your money.' She picks up the tray and hands it to him. 'And you look very smart,' she murmurs.

An hour later, the manager of The White Hart is also telling Mark how smart he looks. The manager, Mr Colman, is a large man, whose cheeks are such a ripe red that he always reminds Mark of a ventriloquist's dummy. 'Now, Mark,' he says, 'I want you to welcome the young people to the under-eighteen club and don't forget to tell them that for this week only, it's half-price to get in and give them one of these leaflets. Then, Ed will take over,' he points at the bulky bodyguard at the entrance, who waves a hand at Mark. For as long as Mark can remember, bodyguards have been the enemy, determined to keep him out of even the humblest of nightclubs. But suddenly, now they're allies, working together. 'Ed will also keep out any shady people,' says the manager. He makes it sound as if shady people are instantly recognisable. 'Then, when everyone's in, about half seven, come up and circulate at the disco, then around nine o'clock we'll get you to start the Karaoke. Mark nods. The manager digs into his pocket and waves a five pound note at Mark. 'This is to buy the lassies a drink, make them feel at home. All right, Mark?'

'Yes, fine.'

'Good man,' says the manager. 'I'll see you later then.' He leaves Mark stamping his feet with the cold. This must be the coldest night since the Ice Age; and Mark is absolutely freezing. His mum was right, he should have worn a coat. It's just that he hasn't got a decent coat and he wanted everyone to get a good view of the suit.

He paces around, hands in his pockets, then his eyes glint with astonishment – and pleasure. Becky is walking towards him. But she and the others aren't due for another hour yet. 'Come in, little girl,' he says. 'This is a surprise,' he adds. 'Recovered from last night, then?'

'Just about.'

'I came home to find my dad doing handstands in the lounge, all the neighbours were there. Talk about embarrassing.' She smiles faintly. 'Anything wrong, Becky?'

'No, nothing really, except, well Adam's just rung

me. His parents have invited me to go with them to the synagogue next Saturday.'

'That's good, isn't it?'

'Oh, I don't think so. I mean, his parents are out to break us up. I think this is a trap. They're going to do something. Only I don't know what.'

Mark considers this. 'Have you said anything to Adam?'

'No, because a couple of days ago I had a bit of a go at him about his family and he started defending them. He said, it's nothing against me, it's just what they believe. It's like Cathy not wanting to marry a meat-eater.'

'They are his family, I suppose,' says Mark.

'I know and I'm afraid, Mark. They're going to win, aren't they?'

He puts an arm around her. 'I'd go,' he says, 'but get Adam to coach you first, tell you everything you've got to do so they can't catch you out. Like, I know, women have to have their arms covered.' He gazes down at her legs. 'And their legs too, I think.'

Two girls approach. 'Are you for the under-eighteens' club?' asks Mark.

'That's right,' says the taller girl. 'And you're Mark, aren't you?'

He smiles, hands them a leaflet and says, 'Just go right along in. You're the first to arrive, actually. There's a free drink because it's the first week and tickets are only a pound.' The girls start opening their purses. 'No, you pay upstairs,' he says, 'though you can give me some money too, if you like.'

The girls laugh, then the taller one says, 'See you later then, Mark.'

Mark shakes his head. 'Don't know how they knew my name. I'm sure I've never met them. Everyone seems to know me, these days.'

'You're becoming famous, Mark,' says Becky. And as she looks at him, just for a second there, she almost fancies him. For he does look especially cute tonight. 'You've done really well, haven't you, Mark?'

'You reckon.'

'Yes. I mean, you're singing all over the place. You're organising the Comic Relief day at college, you're doing this . . .'

'Suddenly, I'm someone. And when you've spent most of your life being a joke . . .' he kicks at a stone, 'makes a change.'

Becky gives him a light, spontaneous kiss. 'And you're right,' she says, 'I shall go to the synagogue with Adam's family and I will get Adam to coach me beforehand. But I'll still be the outsider, won't I? And Mark, I'm dreading it.'

5 Hotel Booking for a Convict

Becky follows Adam's mum up the steps of the synagogue. When Adam first told her that only the men were allowed downstairs and that all the women were banished upstairs, Becky had erupted. 'But that's sexist,' she'd cried. To which Adam had said mildly, 'Not really. It's no big deal. It's just a custom.'

But as Becky and his mum are shown into their seat, near the front of the gallery, Becky can't help saying to herself, 'But this is sexist. It is.' Most of the women here are, like Adam's mum, wearing hats which means they're married, doesn't it? That was one of about a thousand facts Adam had told her last night. A few of the women nod and smile at her. Then, she hears Adam's mum say, 'Yes, this is Becky, Adam's friend.' Her voice has a slightly singsong quality as if she's been practising saying this. Maybe she has. Becky feels suddenly self-conscious, very much the new girl. At least her clothes are right: smartish, dullish, very respectable.

The women are whispering away, although the service seems to have already started. She looks down at a choir (all male, of course) in full voice. Then she sees Adam gazing up anxiously at her.

He's searching her face for that little gleam in her eye which is almost always there. Yes, there it is and she's smiling – but it's an exhausted smile. Is that surprising? All last night he was cramming facts into her and she was so anxious to "get it right". But now, he feels ashamed. Why is he making her go through this? It's because of his parents, of course. They said how 'nice' it would be if he brought Becky along to a service – and then they kept on saying it. Until Adam thought, here's a chance to please them for a change, but really it's not fair on Becky. He'll never ask her to do this again. Then he sees his mother whisper something to Becky.

Adam's mum says, 'There's the rabbi, Becky,' and she points to a man wearing a long black gown standing by a podium. 'And there's the cantor . . .' Becky's gaze moves upwards to what looks like an old lantern held up by a single chain. 'And that,' says Adam's mum, 'is where we keep the eternal flame.' She says it quite proudly too, as if she were showing off something which belonged to her. In a way, Becky supposes it does.

Now Adam's mum is pointing out other things, but Becky keeps returning to that eternal flame. She thinks of all those people who must have sat and stared at that flame and in two centuries time, when everyone here is, as Mark would put it, food for worms, people will still be seeing what Becky's seeing now. Suddenly, it's as if the past and the future are here too, woven together in this moment. Perhaps, that's what religion does for people, helps them fit things together, see some kind of pattern. Becky's not at all religious and she can only remember her mum taking her to church once, years ago now. Her dad was there too. It was one Christmas Eve and the church was packed. And her mum kept asking in a loud voice if someone could please open the doors before she suffocated.

Becky hardly knows anything about the Bible. She always hated RE at school. Yet, last night, when Adam was rattling off all this stuff about the Covenant and Torah . . . Well, it's absurd to be jealous of a religion but she was, just a little. For even though he's always criticising it, that religion is still there, a part of him. It's like a girlfriend he's finished with but can't quite forget.

She looks for Adam. For a second, she can't find him. He's swallowed up by all the men wearing identical black and white prayer shawls. It's a shock to see Adam in that shawl; it's almost as if he's put on a little disguise. Now he isn't the Adam she knows. He's turning into a stranger. Didn't he say when he was younger that he was very religious? So are all those religious feelings flooding back? Are they snatching him away from her? Then suddenly,

102

Adam looks up and winks at her. And Becky laughs at herself for being so absurd.

Two hours later, the service is finally over and Becky is exhausted but quite pleased with herself. She didn't let herself or Adam down once. She feels like an actress who's had a most successful first night.

Outside, the sky looks dark and heavy and it's another bleakly cold day but all around Becky, people are shaking hands and smiling. It's like a huge family reunion and Becky feels very much the outsider. And while in the synagogue, she could just stare ahead at her own thoughts, now she feels rather obviously out of it. Every so often Adam's mother smiles across at her and Adam is fighting his way over but Reuben keeps introducing people to him.

Now Reuben is bringing over a very attractive girl to Adam. And Adam seems to know her because he says something and they both burst out laughing. Becky feels suddenly panicky again. That's the kind of girl for Adam, isn't it? Life would be so much simpler for him if he went out with her. And they seem to be old friends. If only she could hear what they are saying. Should she casually wander over? She's still deciding when a woman with grey hair and glasses suddenly asks, 'So, Becky, where do you live?'

Meanwhile, Adam is still caught in conversation with Natasha. 'No, you haven't changed that much,' she says, 'apart from the fact you're a foot taller. But it's so good to see you again. Now, you are coming on the outing to Bournemouth, aren't you?'

'I don't know,' says Adam.

'Yes, he'll come,' says Reuben. 'Put his name down.'

'Oh, great,' says Natasha. 'I know Bournemouth doesn't sound very exciting, but with the right people . . . See you later then, Adam.'

Adam nods, then pushes Reuben aside. 'What are you doing? You know I hate those Jewish social club outings.'

'Going on one now and again won't hurt,' says Reuben. 'Besides, Natasha is a very nice girl.'

Adam stares hard at Reuben. 'You're in this too, aren't you? You've been briefed, haven't you?'

'What are you talking about?'

'This plan, to break me and Becky up.'

'There is no plan. Look, Adam, I want you to stay friends with Becky. Of course I do. She's a nice girl. But there's no harm in seeing other girls too. You're young, you don't want to get too serious yet, do you?'

'But it is serious, Reuben.'

Reuben's face falls.

'What did you all think, Reuben? One trip to the synagogue, a smile from a pretty girl and it would be goodbye Becky?' Adam shakes his head and walks towards Becky. Then he goes over and kisses her right on the lips.

Becky smiles at him nervously. Then she sees Reuben and Adam's dad coming up behind him and she remembers something; on Thursday when Adam came for tea, he took a picture of Becky with her mum. It was a nice gesture and her mum was rather flattered. Becky decides to return the compliment. She takes out her camera and says, 'Mr and Mrs Rosen, Reuben, I'd like to take a picture of you please, with Adam ... so if you'd all bunch together.' She starts messing about with the camera – it's her mum's actually – and she wants to make certain she presses the right button. Then she looks up again to see that none of Adam's family are moving. Instead, they are staring at her, in varying degrees of horror. She puts the camera down. 'What's wrong?' she gasps. Other people are gathering round and gaping a bit too. She turns to Adam and even he's looking a bit shocked. She can feel herself growing hysterical. 'What have I done wrong, Adam? Tell me.'

'It's nothing,' he says calmly. Too calmly. 'It's just we don't touch anything mechanical on Saturday. That's why we had to walk here . . .'

'But a camera, that's not . . . Oh yes, I suppose it is. I didn't think, I'm so sorry.' Now her voice isn't behaving right. And it seems as if just about everyone is watching her. 'No one told me about cameras. It's not my fault.' She turns away from all those shocked faces, her eyes brimming with tears.

'I should have told you about cameras. It's my fault. It's a stupid rule anyway. It's all so stupid.' He strokes the side of her face, murmuring, 'You were brilliant today, you know.' Becky starts to calm down. 'Want to go?' he asks unexpectedly.

'If you do,' replies Becky.

'Yeah, come on,' he says, gazing right at her. 'For

whatever you do they'll always be against us. They want to break us up, Becky.' His arm is wrapped tightly around her now. 'But I'm never letting you go.'

'I think it's so horrible. We both do.' Cathy turns to Jason, frowning beside her, in dark glasses. 'To walk past your shop and see rabbits just hanging outside, that you haven't even skinned, rabbits with all their fur left on.' Cathy's head is hammering furiously. She'll have an almighty headache any minute now. This always happens when she gets angry. 'I don't see why sex shops have to be all covered up but you're allowed to show as many murdered bodies as you want.'

'You kids don't understand,' says the butcher.

Cathy has a theory, that all butchers are fat and bearded, but he's actually smallish, clean-shaven, with rather faded blonde hair and startlingly white eyebrows. He half smiles.

'I'm not aware the lady has said anything funny,' growls Jason, standing beside Cathy like her personal bodyguard.

'You won't see it, will you?' says the butcher wearily. 'I'm just doing a job, that's all. People like eating meat for their Sunday lunch. They have done, for centuries.'

'For centuries, people had slaves,' snaps Cathy, 'that doesn't make it right.'

'Ah, changing the world, are we?' The butcher waves a contemptuous hand. 'Where's your "ban the bomb" sign, then?' The door pushes open. A woman, holding a little girl, enters.

'Fancy bringing a child in here,' cries Cathy. The woman gives Cathy a quick look. 'Why not try eating something that isn't dead tonight,' Cathy says.

'Ah, go and join a peace march,' says the butcher. He smiles at the woman. 'Sorry about that, Mrs Crompton.'

'Let's beat it, Cathy,' murmurs Jason. 'This isn't doing any good.'

But Cathy bends down to the little girl. 'Did you see those poor rabbits hanging outside? Perhaps you've got a pet rabbit yourself . . .' The woman pulls the little girl away from Cathy and Jason propels Cathy outside.

'I told you arguing doesn't work,' says Jason. Then he sees Cathy is still shaking.

'Can you believe that woman, taking a child in there?'

'Direct action,' says Jason. 'That's the only way.'

'You mustn't smash his window,' says Cathy quickly. 'That won't do any good.'

'Yes, it will, it will put his insurance right up, for a start – and put some fear into him. Come on, that spud's just asking for it.'

'No, Jason, that isn't the way. We'd lose public support straight away. People are starting to change all around us – only not as quickly as we'd like.'

'I tell you, Cathy, if the suffragettes had thought like you, women would still be waiting for the vote.'

She grins. 'But in history, Mr Charlton said it was

all the things women did in the war that got them the vote.'

'Mr Charlton, he wears slip-on shoes, so you can't trust anything he says . . . but all right, I won't smash this guy's windows.'

Cathy's quite surprised by how quickly Jason's given in. 'Thanks, Jason – and thanks for going in with me. Oh, look, there they go.' The woman and the little girl are trailing out of the butcher's shop now and going across the road. 'So what dead animal are you eating tonight?' Cathy calls after them. The girl turns round and stares, until the woman tugs at her hand and they walk quickly away. 'Did you see how guilty that woman looked?' says Cathy.

'She still bought the meat, though,' says Jason. He looks across the road at the sports shop. 'What's keeping Lauren, then?'

'That's the fourth time you've asked me that, not very flattering you know.' Jason laughs, embarrassed. 'I told you, she's photocopying all the notes we missed on *The Rivals*. She'll probably be ages yet.' Cathy had offered to stay behind and do the photocopying but Lauren had insisted.

It's funny how, since she split with Grant, Lauren's popularity at college has risen, especially in their new English group. There's a group of boys who've been especially helpful. Three of them are helping Lauren now.

And Cathy can't blame Lauren for enjoying this new wave of popularity. Or even for flirting with these boys. Lauren has to have her admirers. Yet,

Cathy has already dropped one or two hints to her about "not being too friendly".

'Why don't we go and have a cup of tea somewhere?' asks Cathy. 'We can leave a message at your shop for Lauren, that's if you can bear still more of my company, of course.'

'All right, all right,' says Jason. 'But we're not going to that hole Becky and Mark like.'

'Okay, how about being very posh and going to the tea-rooms, then?'

'The tea-rooms! They have to give all their customers oxygen masks in there, they're so old ... Still, why not, it'll be different.' As he disappears into the sports shop, Cathy sniffs hard. It's the second week of March, almost Spring, and Cathy can actually feel the air growing lighter. Just a few weeks ago, at half past four, the night was already rolling in and it hung over the town like a great heavy fog, muffling all the familiar sights. But now, the fog has finally lifted and Cathy can watch the shop assistants hanging around the doorways as the countdown to closing time starts, (it's at half past five though, that Cathy starts work at the *Pizza Paradiso*, a six-hour shift) while groups of girls hang around the fountain, calling out things to boys. You can tell they are Cartford girls, because they are wearing really high heels with great big plasters across their feet. One or two boys strut around the edges of the girls' conversation. But one boy's already in the centre. It's Mark. Cathy watches him, fascinated, until suddenly, Mark sees her and immediately bounds over.

Mark's dressed in a blazer and smart shirt and trousers. He always dresses up now and is one of the very few students not to wear jeans to college. 'Hey, Cathy,' he says.

'More fans,' says Cathy.

'Well, they like to keep in with the management. And I do a few business deals with them, like, if they bring ten people along I let them in free. Had a hundred and fifty people at the under-eighteens' disco last night. I get commission when we go over one hundred.' He grins, 'Not bad, is it, being chatted up by girls and getting paid for it.'

'I can see you're just lapping it up,' says Cathy.

'Who are you waiting for?' asks Mark.

'Jason,' says Cathy. Mark immediately stands to attention.

'We're going to the tea-rooms, so if you'd like to come along.'

'The tea-rooms? My mum goes in there. Still, if Jason's going. Shame Jason's not coming to Brighton with us tomorrow.'

'Yeah, he's got a little thing called a driving test, tomorrow afternoon.'

'He'll walk it.'

'Unlike me,' says Cathy, 'I'm just dreading it.'

'Well forget it now and think about tomorrow; free travel on the trains and what a crack it's going to be, with you, me, Adam and Becky.' Tomorrow is Comic Relief day and Mark, as one of the college organisers, has got them free train passes to raise money in Brighton.

Now Cathy spots Jason coming out of the sports shop. He always walks as if his shoes have got hidden springs in them but today, to Cathy's surprise, Jason isn't moving with his customary energy. Instead, he's almost slouching. There is something bothering him, isn't there? Is he worrying about his test tomorrow?

'All right, Markie, my old fruit,' says Jason.

'We had one hundred and fifty at the under-eighteens' disco last night, Jas,' says Mark. He pulls Jason's dark glasses off, tries them on and then puts them back on Jason again. 'I'd wear dark glasses,' says Mark, 'only they don't really suit me. My fore-head's too small. Was Tania in the shop, by the way?'

'Yeah, I left her in charge.'

'Right.' Mark considers this. 'Do you think I should go in and see her then, or is it too soon?'

'Too soon?' echoes Cathy questioningly.

Mark says, 'You know Tania's been going out with that guy, Carl, who lives down Becky's road. Well, she and Carl have just broken up. She told Jason yesterday, who rang me.'

'And you want to ask her out,' says Cathy.

Mark twists his face about. 'I might,' he says. 'The thing is, though, Cathy, I don't want to go charging in there like a hot-head and saying "How about it, lazy lips", which is my usual style. Jason reckons I should bide my time and go for the subtle approach.

111

Trouble is, Jason, what exactly is the subtle approach?'

'I'm still working on that one,' says Jason, grinning. 'No, it's going in the back door rather than the front.'

Mark nods. 'Tania's been very friendly to me lately and *I think* now, she does fancy me. But then, sometimes I'm not sure if she isn't too friendly. You know how people are when there are no strings attached. That's why, like Jason says, I'm playing it cool, as I can wait. I'm not looking for a two-week mess-about. I want this to last.' His voice is becoming more and more uncertain. 'If you could tell her that I had one hundred and fifty at the under-eighteens' disco, Jason, it might, you know.'

'Don't worry mate, I will,' says Jason.

'I'll just go and casually look at the new trainers then . . . like I said, I can wait – and there are other girls too. There's this girl at the hairdresser's who fancies me. She always washes my hair three times, when you're only supposed to wash it once. I'll catch you up, then.' He gives them a small smile. 'I hate not knowing if a girl fancies you or not . . . hate it.'

'Oh, poor Mark,' says Cathy, as she and Jason start walking up to the tea-rooms. 'Do you think Tania does like him?'

'I think he could be in there,' says Jason.

'I hope so,' says Cathy, 'because he really wants a girlfriend and as Adam and Becky seem to be getting more and more serious . . . No, I hope it does work out with Tania.'

'What's this about you and Graham, then?' says Jason. 'Lauren said . . .'

'No,' says Cathy at once. 'It's nothing. Believe me, it's just Graham comes into the *Pizza Paradiso* a lot, on his own, so I've gone over and chatted to him, as he looks lonely. Then yesterday, he rang me up just as I was leaving for work and asked if I'd like to go to the Unicorn, his local pub, tomorrow, as he'd be there with his mates. And I didn't fancy walking into a pub I didn't know and sitting with Graham and all his mates, so I was very brave and said, "Thanks, but no thanks." To be honest, Jason, I don't even know if I want to go out with anyone at the moment. I mean, everyone's rushing into couples but I'd rather wait for the right man.' She laughs. 'Famous last words.'

Inside the tea-room an elderly man, in a shirt, tie and waistcoat looks round expectantly. There are two pots of tea on his table and Cathy wonders if he's waiting for his date. In another corner sit two women, hunched over their screaming babies.

'We're sitting right away from that,' says Jason. A beaming woman with shoulder-length grey hair takes their order, then Jason yawns loudly. 'Sorry,' he says, then he yawns again. 'I'm knackered.'

'Might I ask why?' asks Cathy. She reaches across, pulling his glasses off. 'I hate talking to you when I can't see your eyes. That's better. But yes, you do look tired. You're not worrying over the test tomorrow, are you?'

'No, not at all. It's just, I didn't sleep too well last night. I . . .' he hesitated.

'Come on, spit it out.'

He taps his spoon against the cup. 'Cathy, do you remember when I thought I dreamt of my own funeral?'

'How could I forget that? You said how you saw us inside a church, dressed in black and masses of other people from school were there . . . In fact, everyone was, except you. And for weeks afterwards . . .'

'Yeah, yeah,' interrupts Jason, 'and then Adam's girlfriend died, and you all went to the funeral – only I couldn't because I had really bad flu. So it wasn't my funeral I'd seen . . . Remember?'

'Yes,' says Cathy doubtfully. She certainly remembers all the hours they'd spent in the hut discussing Jason's dream. And it both fascinated and alarmed her. It was like discovering that behind the mirror we stare through every day, where everything's so safe, so sane, so dull, in fact, lies another mirror, of which we gain only the briefest flashes, often when we're least expecting them.

She picks up the tea-pot. Funny, how all of life's mysteries vanish when you're brandishing a tea-pot. And how cloyingly cosy tea sounds when it is poured into a cup. 'There you go,' she says to Jason. 'I'll let you put in your usual nineteen sugars.' Then, while she's stirring her own tea – another reassuring sound – she says, 'Yes, but Jason, you dreamt about that funeral months before . . . and we were in a synagogue, not a church. And there was no one else

114

from our school there . . .' Cathy gazes across at a woman munching away with obvious relish at her toasted tea-cake. But even so, there's a definite tremor in her voice when she asks, 'You haven't had another dream, have you?'

'As it happens, I have.'

'Not another funeral?'

He shakes his head. 'Cathy, if I tell you, you must promise not to . . .'

'Yes, of course I will.' She takes a deep breath, 'Even though it's all nonsense,' she whispers to herself.

Jason snatches up his dark glasses and puts them back on. 'I dreamt that Lauren and I finished. I caught her kissing another bloke. Then she looked over at me and I knew it was over.' His voice is deliberately flat and unemotional but Cathy knows he's shaken too. For Jason believes in things like this.

Cathy doesn't. Well, not really. It's hard not to, a little, isn't it? Behind Cathy, the man in the waistcoat is stumbling to his feet. He is breathing heavily and then lets out a sigh that seems to echo in Cathy's ear. 'But one dream,' begins Cathy.

Jason interrupts. 'Cathy, it isn't the first time I've had that dream.'

Cathy hesitates – but no – she must be factual about this. 'Dreams mean nothing, how can they? It's all nonsense.'

Yet, Jason doesn't appear to hear. For he goes on. 'What I remember most, though, is thinking that I had everything I wanted. I had it right there, in my hand . . . and then I lost it all.'

Mark puts the phone down, shocked by what he's just heard. Then, slowly picks up the huge pink head, eases it on again, and walks out of the telephone box.

Outside, Adam, who is wearing a shirt and trousers with arrows painted all over them, funny canvas shoes and a balloon on a piece of string around his ankles, is pinning Comic Relief stickers on to two small children. Yet, as soon as they see Mark, they race over.

'It's the Pink Panther,' cries the little girl and they both start dancing behind Mark, singing the Pink Panther song.

'So what are your names, then?' asks Mark.

They stare at him, suddenly shy, until the little girl bursts out, 'I'm Lucy and he's Ben.'

Mark picks up his collection box. 'Lucy and Ben, my box is practically full. If you put some money in, it will be full.' They immediately rush over to their mother, begging for money for the pink panther.

'Come on, Mum,' calls Mark. 'It's for a good cause.' So each of the children is given fifty pence worth of change and as a reward Mark lets them both pull his tail as hard as they can, before their mother finally drags them away.

'We're doing all right today, aren't we?' says Adam. Then he asks, 'How did Jason get on?'

Mark hesitates. 'I didn't speak to Jas, he was out,

so I don't know what went on but his mum reckons he's failed.' Even now, his tone is disbelieving. The words, "Jason" and "fail" don't belong in the same paragraph, never mind the same sentence. Mark's tone becomes bitter. 'How could anyone fail Jason? He's a brilliant driver and he's done up that car. I'm ringing Jas when we get back.' He looks at his watch. 'You won't believe the time. It only feels about six o'clock, doesn't it? It's actually just gone eight o'clock.'

They both gaze down the Brighton sea front at the people streaming past. Even though it is a dull, drizzly evening, there is a definite buzz, a sense of life stretching on in to the evening.

'I wish we could stay on longer,' says Mark, 'but our passes run out at . . . actually, if we're going to catch the 8.40, we'd better get going pretty soon, hadn't we?' Adam nods glumly. As it is a Friday night, he'd promised his parents he'd be home by six o'clock. In fact, if they catch the 8.40, it will be after midnight before he gets home, by which time his parents will be nicely stressed.

As it is, hardly a night goes by when Adam doesn't hear a sudden ominous creak outside his door. That's when he knows his parents are standing guard again, making sure there are no more escape bids. And during the evening, although his parents never say he can't see Becky, they make a big deal out of his homework; 'Becky will understand why you can't go out tonight,' they say.

And even Becky's mum is becoming much stricter

about what time Becky gets in. Time . . . all Adam and Becky's meetings seem bound by time now. An hour snatched here, half an hour there. No real time at all.

It's then it hits him. An idea so simple and yet so brilliant – why don't he and Becky stay over in Brighton tonight? After all, he's going to get mighty hassle from his parents anyway, so what's he got to lose. Why not?

His mind is jumping about, turning somersaults. Where can they stay? On the beach? No, far too cold. They'll need rooms, well, one room. He gives a little shiver of excitement. So how much money has he got? Just by chance, he happens to have a month's wages from the video shop on him, including over-time. So that should pay for a cheapish room and the fare back. He can't keep still now, he's so excited. What's Mark saying, something about getting the girls. 'Yes, I'll go get the girls,' says Adam.

He sprints the few yards into the pub. It's small and smoky with disco music blasting out. Adam spots Becky right away. It's hard to miss her. She's wearing the most disgusting pink dress she could find at Oxfam, matched only in awfulness by her massive red leggings and silver boots.

'Come on, be generous now, stick a fiver in there,' cries Becky. 'It's all for a good cause.' Then, up pops Cathy in a patterned top, a long purple skirt and different coloured leggings, waving another collection box. They both seem to be enjoying themselves. It's funny how self-conscious they felt at first about collecting money, they were all just so timidly polite. But now, they've learnt you get more money if you're a little cheeky and can have a joke with people. Then a voice calls, 'Got another one in here now.' Becky and Cathy immediately look up and Adam signals for them to join him outside.

Adam's having doubts about his idea now. Where would they stay, for instance? He and Becky don't want to waste time trailing around hotels half the night. There was a place he saw, a bit further up, down one of the side streets, that had a large board outside saying, "Out of season rates. Single room twenty five pounds, double room, forty pounds." So if he could find that place . . .

Now they are all outside the pub, putting their collection boxes in to Mark's sports bag and talking about Jason. They're about to start going back. So he'll have to speak up now and ask Becky if she wants to . . . in front of Mark and Cathy. Unless he asks if he could speak to Becky alone. No, that'll be even more embarrassing.

'I tell you, she's a prostitute, isn't she, Adam?' asks Mark.

Adam starts. 'Who?' Then he sees Mark is pointing at a woman brushing her hair in the photo-booth. He shrugs his shoulders.

'Just because she's brushing her hair, you're saying she's a prostitute?' says Cathy.

'No, no, she's waiting for a customer,' says Mark.

'Mark knows about these things,' teases Becky.

Mark's blushing now, while Adam's thinking this

clearly isn't the right moment to put his proposal to Becky. But Cathy's saying, 'Well, we'd better go if we're going to catch the 8.40. Can we go back via the beach?' Adam's chance is slipping away. He must ask Becky to wait . . . but she's already linked arms with Cathy. Now they're crossing the road.

'Come on, Adam,' calls Mark.

Adam turns round and points to the large hotel behind him. 'I'm just going to the loo,' he says. 'I'll catch you up.' Becky's turning round questioningly and Mark's repeating what he just said. Then Adam stands at the top of the steps watching them, until they disappear out of sight.

Next, he charges down the steps again and runs as fast as he can. For he's decided to check out this hotel for himself. After that, he'll . . . Well, one step at a time, as they say. First, he's got to find this hotel. Was it down this street or further down? No, there it is. Hard to miss that sign. He stands reading it again, his heart thumping. So the forty pounds includes a full English breakfast, that's quite good, isn't it? Well, go inside and book it up, then. Come on, Adam, stop being wimpy, do it. He pulls down the hood of his costume, walks up the path and presses the doorbell. Almost at once the door is opened by a small, red-cheeked woman, who looks rather like an elderly pixie.

'Er, sorry to bother you, but have you got any rooms left for tonight?' Then, in case she's wondering why he's roaming around dressed in a convict costume, he says, 'I'm doing Comic Relief.'

She smiles. 'Yes. Come on in. Still raining, is it?'

'Just a bit, yes.' He wipes his shoes on the mat. The hall is dark and dim and, looming over you, is the staircase, stretching off into infinity. But from the door which is marked 'lounge' comes the sound of a television blaring and someone bellowing with laughter.

'One night, is it?' asks the woman.

'Yes, please.'

'Single?'

'A double. My – partner is on her way.'

'Fine, if you will just sign the book here, please, sir,' and she opens a large red book on the desk and hands Adam a pen. He signs, Adam Rosen, as boldly as he can. Behind them comes another roar of laughter. 'We've got your Comic Relief on now,' says the woman. 'That's the lounge, by the way, which guests are free to use at any time. Would you like to see your room?'

'No, it's all right, I'll go and get my partner first.'

'All right. Well, there's the key to your room, number twelve, and there's the outside door key. Just press that button,' she points to a button on the desk, 'if you need anything.'

'Thank you, thank you very much,' says Adam. He feels a sudden burst of excitement as he takes the keys. He's got the room, and so easily.

Images flash through his head; he and Becky getting up, and sitting on the beach together, watching the dawn rise. Then, instead of sneaking back to their houses, they can walk back together and then . . . he sees Becky lying in bed, bathed in light. He hears her hair swish on the pillow as she turns over to kiss him . . . and then a jumble of images, all running into each other until his heart's racing so fast he thinks he'll explode. He should stop running, but he can't. It's as if he's suddenly been plunged into overdrive.

He's like those moths, who, when you switch on a light, just dive towards it and then they go spinning around the room, drunk with ecstasy.

Now he's scrunching his way over the beach. He calls out to them. They're still a long way ahead. No one hears him. Then he calls again. This time, Becky turns round and he hurtles towards her, just like he did the morning after their first date.

'You've been ages,' says Mark.

'I'm not going back,' says Adam, still gasping for breath. 'I'm staying here tonight. I've booked a room.' He wants to add, 'For us,' but instead just waves the keys in the air. They're all deathly silent as if they can't believe what he's just said. This is definitely the most embarrassing moment of Adam's life.

Then Cathy asks, 'Want us to get lost for a minute?' and without waiting for an answer half pulls Mark down the beach.

Becky doesn't move towards Adam. She just asks coldly, 'So how long has this been planned?' What is Adam doing just springing this on her? He should have talked to her about it, long before now. Something like this is a joint decision.

'It wasn't planned. I just did it, spur of the moment.'

Becky nods but she's still really taken aback by all this. And nervous. Even though she must have spent hundreds of hours alone with Adam, this is different. Now there's a bedroom. So just what is he expecting?

As if he can read her thoughts, Adam says, 'I just thought it would give us more time together, so we can be on our actual own.' I didn't get the room, he was going to add, for that reason, only that sounds funny. 'I don't expect anything. I mean, what comes out of it, comes out of it . . . it's just time to be on our own.' He looks terminally embarrassed and his left hand is shaking. Becky starts to relax. He's booked the room because he wants to be with her, that's all. So what's wrong with that? Nothing.

She looks at him, then says with a sly smile, 'You booked a room dressed like that?'

'Just wait till they see you,' he says. She giggles again, while the idea of tonight grows in her head. All of a sudden, booking that room seems like a brilliant idea. But she's not sure what to say; 'Let's get to it' doesn't seem quite right. So, in the end, she just walks over to Adam and stands beside him, almost as if they were forming teams. Then she calls out, 'We're going to stay over, then.' Mark and Cathy turn round. They hurry up the beach towards them. Cathy is staring hard at Becky while Becky smiles back at her as if to say, 'Yes, it's all right.'

'Okay then,' says Cathy. 'Well, it's certainly a

lovely place to stay over – better than dreary old Cartford any day, isn't it, Mark?'

Mark takes off the pink panther's head. His face is stern and unsmiling. 'So you're not coming back with us? You're breaking up this happy party.' There's a definite edge of sarcasm in his voice as he says this. 'Well, that's a real slap in the face for Cathy and me, isn't it?'

'It's only tonight,' says Becky. 'We'll see you tomorrow, Mark.'

Mark shrugs his shoulders. 'Stay as long as you like.'

'Anyway, Mark,' says Cathy briskly, 'we've got a train to catch, so we'd better go.' Cathy goes over to Becky and Adam and gives them both a brief hug. 'Bye then,' says Cathy. She and Becky exchange awkward smiles. Then Becky and Adam call, 'Goodbye,' to Mark. He just waves his hand dismissively and mutters, 'Sleep well.'

Adam and Becky watch them go. Then Becky gives a little shiver.

'Cold?' asks Adam.

'Just a bit.'

He immediately puts his arm around her. 'You, we, don't have to stay.'

'But I want to,' she says firmly. She smiles. 'Now stop gassing and show me our room.'

6 Cathy Wins – and Loses

'You may start the car now, Miss Adams.' Cathy's legs start shaking again. In the waiting room, Cathy's legs were shaking so much she was convinced she wouldn't be able to stand up. Her examiner would appear and she'd just belly-flop in front of him. And when she saw him he was the image of her old head-master; same musty suit, same grave voice, same way of breathing heavily through his nose and probably the same hair growing out of his ears. She darts a glance at him. He's looking down at his clipboard.

Every mistake she makes is going to be written down and used in evidence against her, isn't it? How many mistakes are you allowed? Only three, isn't it? Thinking about this makes Cathy so nervous she immediately slams the handbreak off and the car does its impression of a kangaroo. He looks up. 'I'm sorry,' says Cathy. He doesn't say anything. He doesn't even give a little smile. It's probably against the law for him to smile, isn't it?

'Now just follow the road ahead, interpreting the road signs, unless I direct you otherwise, Miss Adams.' Then he leans over and writes something down on his clipboard. She wonders how many points she's going to lose for slamming the handbrake. That was his fault, really. He made her nervous. It's like when you're in an exam and the teacher stands behind you, looking at what you've just written; at once, you seize up, don't you? She could drive much better if he weren't in the car with her. And anyway, why is she doing this? She hasn't even got a car. So just what is she trying to prove? She's not sure. It's just something she wants to do, a target she has set herself. At one time she thought she was doing this to prove something to Giles, show him how successful she is, but actually, it's herself she's really got to convince.

Cathy's starting to feel hot. Dare she ask him if she can open a window? She finally dares, when she's driving back into the test-centre and the sweat is just rolling down her face (and she knows her face is flaming red), she gasps, 'Do you mind if I open a window, please?'

'Certainly not,' he says. 'I think we're both rather hot.'

Wow. He's being a teeny bit nice, isn't he? Or did he mean that her driving was making him sweat as well? Certainly he lurched forward after Cathy's emergency stop and for one awful moment she thought he was going to fly right through the windscreen. No wonder he said, 'I will not ask you to do

126

that again.' But overall, she feels her driving improved as she went along. But it's impossible to know what he's thinking: every time she looked at him he was either frowning down at his clipboard or picking the dirt out of his nails.

They go through the highway code questions. Cathy's quite confident here as Lauren has tested her several times. But all the time she's getting more and more nervous. Any minute she'll find out . . . Well, if she's failed she doesn't want a long post-mortem of all the things she did wrong. She'd rather he just told her and left.

Now there's a pause. Is this the end of the highway code questions? Then he says, 'I am pleased to inform you that you have reached the required standard . . .' His tone is so formal that his words don't sink in at first. Then she exclaims 'I've passed!' and there is just the merest flicker of a smile as he says, 'Congratulations, Miss Adams.'

'Thank you, thank you!' Cathy goes to get out of the car. 'Oh no, you get out, don't you,' she cries, more flustered than ever. He gives another faint smile before disappearing. Then Cathy's driving instructor puffs into view. He thumps down beside Cathy, exclaiming, 'Well, that was a surprise, wasn't it?' He also insists on driving Cathy back to town, claiming she's 'too excited' to drive.

But nothing can dampen Cathy's enthusiasm. She bounds across the town centre. Now, who can she tell? She looks at her watch. Lauren and everyone will be in lessons for another quarter of an hour yet.

And she's got to tell someone before then. If only Jez were here. But there's Jason. At once, she's speeding off to the sports shop. As she walks inside she hears a guy saying to Tania, 'I'd like Jason to serve me please,' and immediately Jason glides into view in his track suit. 'I wanted your advice on some running shoes, Jason,' says the guy. Jason goes off with the guy to the footwear section, one of Jason's specialities, while Cathy's jumping up and down impatiently, willing the guy to go.

Finally, when the guy is parading up and down in his new running shoes, Cathy hisses, 'Jason.' He immediately comes over. 'Jason, you won't believe this, I've passed.'

'Oh good,' he says.

'Well, let's have a bit more enthusiasm,' she says.

'I think you've got enough for both of us. No, well done, that's great.'

In all her excitement, Cathy wonders if she's been a bit tactless. After all, Jason failed his driving test and he's never really told them what happened. Just said the examiner hated him. But then, that's so typical of him. Cathy's been keeping an eye on Jason ever since he told her about his dream of Lauren and him splitting up. More than once, she's asked him if he's had any more dreams and every time he says, 'No, not really,' and changes the subject, which has upset Cathy. For that day in the tea-rooms she felt he was really opening up to her and that he needed her – and she's very keen to help him. But now, he's keeping her at a distance again. Sometimes she thinks Jason is the most frustrating person she's ever met. And the most fascinating.

'No, that's great news, Cathy,' says Jason.

She laughs, embarrassed. 'All I need now is a car.'

The customer is calling Jason again. 'Got to go,' he says, 'but we'll go out and celebrate tonight.'

'See you later, then.'

Cathy arrives at college just as Lauren is going into the refectory. Cathy calls out, 'Lauren!' and Lauren yells, 'You've passed, haven't you?' and all at once Lauren is giving her a huge hug. 'Oh, that's really great,' she cries. She turns round to three guys who are following her (Cathy calls them Lauren's fan club), 'Cathy's passed her driving test, first time, too.'

'Yeah, we worked that one out,' says one of the guys. But now, they're calling out, 'Congratulations,' while Cathy and Lauren link arms and walk to the refectory.

'I was convinced I was going to fail, you know,' says Cathy. 'I just wasn't confident.'

'I thought you'd pass,' says Lauren.

'You were the only one,' says Cathy. 'I just told Jason by the way, and he said we ought to have a bit of a celebration, tonight.'

'Too right,' says Lauren. 'And it'll be good to get him out. All he wants to do is stay in and watch videos now. He doesn't even want to go to the pub any more.'

Inside the refectory Cathy sees Mark by the coffee machines. 'Mark,' she cries, 'I've passed!'

'Yes!' yells Mark so loudly, that half the refectory turn round. But for once, Cathy isn't the least embarrassed by the attention. She wants it written in great blazing letters across the sky; CATHY ADAMS HAS PASSED HER DRIVING TEST.

At home, her mum says how proud she is and gives her a cheque for one hundred pounds to put towards a car; Giles just gives her a fake smile. Then Lauren rings up to say that there's a change of plan and everyone's meeting up at Jason's at eight o'clock.

Cathy's a few minutes early but Lauren, Mark, Adam and Becky are all there already, leaning against Jason's car. When he bought it, both Cathy and Lauren thought he'd been done. That car was so run-down, it looked beyond hope. But now, after about a thousand hours of work on it, it's transformed. The car's a pale blue colour with black wheels, while inside Jason has put in his huge old-fashioned radio. The seats are not exactly swish, they're really low down and, to be honest, not especially comfortable, and when Jason puts the heating on there's a smell like a chinese take-away. Yet, it's still amazingly impressive and just gleams and shines with all the loving care Jason has put into it. And now Jason himself appears, waving a large white envelope, which he hands to Cathy.

'Oh, cards already, thank you.'

'I bought it before,' says Lauren. 'See, I had confidence in you.'

Cathy opens the card and is just taking in all the

130

funny messages when a key jumps out at her. 'What's this?' she cries.

'I think you can guess that one,' says Jason. Cathy looks up and sees everyone is smiling, and staring at Jason's car.

'Oh no,' gasps Cathy, 'but . . .'

'It's no good to me, at the moment. And anyway, I'm doing up an Alfa Sud, that'll be flasher than this one. So it's yours, take it.'

'But I can't,' splutters Cathy. 'I must give you something. Look, I've got a cheque for one hundred pounds in my bag, for a start.'

Jason waves her cheque away airily. 'We'll do that later,' he says. 'You're taking us out for a drive now.'

'I am? I mean, yes, sure. Will everyone fit in?'

'Oh sure,' says Jason. 'I'm sitting in the front,' he adds, 'as I'm navigating. One of you lucky girls can sit on my lap.'

So Mark, Becky and Adam squash in the back while Lauren perches herself on Jason's lap, in the front.

Cathy looks round. 'Why's Mark got his fingers crossed?'

'Oh, no reason,' grins Mark. 'I feel very safe.'

Then Cathy turns to Jason. 'You know what always ruined parties for me? Worrying how I was going to get back. I'd spend hours creeping around all the people at the party who had cars and they'd all say, 'We'd like to give you a lift but . . .' So in the end I'd ring up my mum and she'd say, 'But I'm in bed,' and then I'd stand outside, waiting for her, knowing she'd be in a really foul mood, but now, thanks to you, Jason, I'm free of all that.' She gazes right at him. 'But are you sure?'

'Just start your car up,' he says.

'Well I'll drive you home, I'll drive you all home from every party,' says Cathy.

'You want to be careful you don't become a taxi service,' says Adam.

'Oh, I don't care about that,' declares Cathy, 'I'm just so . . .'

'Will you stop talking, Cathy, and let's just go somewhere,' interrupts Mark.

Cathy starts up the car. 'Okay, where are we going, then?' she asks.

'Anywhere,' says Jason. 'Just start driving – and we'll stop when we see something interesting.'

'We could be driving all night, then,' says Lauren.

'That's cool,' says Jason. 'Because it's all ours now.' He grins, 'Go for it, Cathy.'

'Go away,' cries Lauren, glaring at her face in the hall mirror. Her mum appears from the kitchen. 'Who are you talking to?'

'This horrible, witching boil, which I know is going to grow and grow . . .'

'No, it won't, if you leave it alone. You've always had good skin, you take after my side of the family for that.' Then she adds, 'Your father'll be right down so make sure you're ready.'

'I'm ready, practically,' cried Lauren. Her dad is driving her to the sports centre, where she's going to watch Jason in the local swimming trials. It's then the doorbell rings. 'I'll go,' says Lauren. She opens the door on Cathy. 'Oh, hi,' says Lauren, more than a little flatly. Why on earth is Cathy visiting her now? She knows Lauren is going out.

And Cathy immediately starts backing away. 'Sorry, you're going out, aren't you?'

'Yes, I'm watching Jason . . .'

'That's right. Look, I'm sorry. I forgot. Catch you later, perhaps. Bye.' She is about to go, when Lauren pulls her back inside.

'Cathy, something's wrong, isn't it? Come on, tell me.'

Cathy nods. 'Something awful's happened.'

Behind her, Lauren can sense her parents hovering within earshot. Should she propel Cathy into the lounge? But there's no time, for Cathy is already saying, 'Mum told me tonight that she and that sleazeball have got engaged.' Just saying the words make her throat tighten. 'They're going to get married in July.' If she says any more, her throat will crack open. So she just looks at Lauren, who immediately begins guiding her into the lounge. 'Oh, sit down here, darling,' says Lauren. Cathy falls down on to the sofa, then gasps, 'I couldn't believe it when she told me.' She rubs her hand over her face, 'I always thought one day she'd see him for what he really is. You hate him too, don't you?'

'Yes, I do,' says Lauren, who's actually only spoken to Giles twice. He was quite smart (well-tailored suits) and younger looking than she'd supposed, bullish, hearty, with a droopy moustache, a kind of ageing medallion man.

'As soon as I went in,' says Cathy, 'I knew something was wrong. Mum was setting the table, saying it was a special meal tonight. Then he came in and stood beside her and she told us.' Cathy's voice quivers, 'and she said it all, bright and larky and my little sister cheered and soon they were all kissing each other while I just sat there. I couldn't look at them, especially not him. I knew he'd just be so pleased with himself. Now he really is king of our house, isn't he?

'Oh, I wouldn't say that,' begins Lauren.

'Yes, he is. He's won, Lauren,' she frowns. 'What really upset me, is that Mum said, to celebrate, we were going to have a four-course meal, starting with prawns.' She stares at Lauren, significantly.

'But you hate prawns,' says Lauren.

'Exactly,' cries Cathy. 'But when I told my mum, she just said, "Oh, with all this excitement, I must have forgotten." That's when I got up and left. I thought, if she's even forgotten that . . . How could she forget that?' Cathy stops. Lauren's father is in the doorway and attempting to cough politely. He sounds more like an elephant psyching itself up for a rampage. 'Your mother and I are about to have some tea,' he says. 'Would you like some?'

Lauren says, 'I won't but Cathy will, won't you?'

'If it's not putting you out,' says Cathy.

'Not at all,' proclaims Lauren's father, before leaving as noisily as he'd arrived.

'You're going to have to go in a minute,' says Cathy.

'No, I won't bother,' she half-laughs. 'It's only Jason, posing about.' But Cathy senses Lauren is really torn. Cathy decides to make it easier for Lauren.

'No, I insist you go and support Jason,' she says. 'He will understand.'

'Yes,' says Cathy slowly, 'I think he will. Actually, if you hadn't been in he'd have been the next person I'd have tried. If you go to him for help, well, he's always got time for you.'

Lauren nods. 'On his own, he's totally different, isn't he? You can tell him all your problems and you feel he really listens. He's just so funny, though. Last night he was going on and on about how he's going to get these two Dobermans and he's going to call them, what was it, Zeus and Apollo. He's totally crazy.'

'You're very lucky to have him, though,' says Cathy unexpectedly. 'To have someone like that, always there for you, that's almost everything, isn't it?'

'Yes,' says Lauren. 'I suppose it is. Sometimes he annoys me, though. Like when we go to a pub, he goes all funny if anyone even says, "Hello" to me. And I'm having a real job to persuade him to go to the Easter party at college next week. He keeps saying "it'll just be a greasy lads' night out".' She stops. 'But never mind all that. I'm sorry, me rattling on . . .'

'No, it's good to think about something else. Lauren, just before you go, I want to ask you a favour.'

'Anything.'

'Well, before I left, I packed a few things ... they're in my car.'

'Oh, right.'

'So could I stay in your bedroom while you're gone, because I can't go back?'

'Of course. It'll be really good having you to stay again.'

'Thanks, Lauren. Now off you go.'

'Are you sure? I feel awful just leaving you like this.'

'No, honestly. I'll be fine.'

Lauren gets up and as if on cue, Lauren's parents appear, Lauren's mum placing a silver tray containing a cup of tea and a plate full of biscuits on the coffee table.

'Cathy's going to stay in my room until I get back,' announces Lauren.

'If that's all right?' says Cathy, giving them her brave little waif smile. She cringes as she does it; it seems as if she's touting for sympathy. In a way she is. For these are proper parents. She immediately feels a rush of envy. Perhaps they'll offer to adopt Cathy; she and Lauren are closer than most sisters already. She imagines telling her mother, 'It's all right, I have a new set of proper parents now.' She knows she's thinking utter rubbish but it's oddly comforting rubbish.

'Well, you're very welcome to stay here with us,' says Lauren's father. 'We're not very exciting, but we've got quite a collection of videos,' and he points to what Jez would call, 'an old granny cabinet.' Lauren's house is full of them. Once Cathy had found all this elderly furniture rather austere and forbidding, but now it suddenly seems reassuring, safe, something to hold on to.

'That would be lovely,' she says.

'We'll let Cathy pick,' says Lauren's mum. 'Have a ladies' night.'

'Ganging up on me, eh,' says Lauren's dad, winking at Cathy. He's always had a soft spot for her. After her father died, he'd said she could always come and talk to him.

'Cathy dear, do you want to just ring your mother, so she knows you're safe?' asks Lauren's mum.

'No,' says Cathy, shortly.

'Ah, I see.' Lauren's mum starts to flutter. 'Well, how would it be, Cathy, if I had a little word with her.'

'Okay,' says Cathy.

'Splendid. Well I'll do that shortly, then. Are you ready now, Lauren?'

'Just got to get my bag,' says Lauren, darting off after her mum, while Lauren's dad eases his layers of stomachs on to the sofa, beside Cathy.

'You know, Cathy, what I think the trouble is in so many homes today is people don't talk to each other. Now, in this house, I like everyone to talk. We say what's bothering us, get it all out in the open. I'm not giving you advice, mind, but maybe if you sat down and talked to your mother. Well, you could start by telling her about those prawns . . .'

'Okay, Dad, I'm ready,' Lauren rushes back in. 'And I think Cathy just wants to sit quietly, actually.'

'I understand,' rumbles Lauren's dad, back on his feet again. 'It's good to think for a while, provided you don't brood. You don't want to do that because life belongs to the doer . . . You have a look through those videos then, Cathy. You're in charge, tonight. I'll get the car out then, Lauren.'

'Okay, Dad.' She smiles at Cathy.

'Wish Jason good luck for me,' says Cathy.

'I will.'

'And you can tell him about . . . I won't mind.'

Lauren looks at Cathy, feeling a sudden stab of sympathy for her. She puts her bag down again and gives Cathy a quick hug. Then she says, 'Cathy, everything's going to be all right,' and then, in case that sounds too facile, she goes on, 'remember you've always got me – and all the others. We'll never desert you.' She gets up. 'See you soon.'

'Good morning, Cathy.' How often has her mum said that to her, but never as formally or as nervously as she says it today, in Lauren's kitchen. Lauren and her mother have disappeared, even though Lauren was only half-way through her breakfast. 'Muffins, eh,' says Cathy's mum, looking at her plate. 'They look nice. We'll have to get some.' She's perched at the opposite end of the table to Cathy, her hair hanging loosely around her face. 'We missed you last night,' she says.

"We," it's always flaming "we." It's as if her mum isn't a whole person any more. Even when she sent Cathy a congratulations card for passing her driving test, she had to write, 'with love from Mum and Giles.' Why couldn't the card have just been from her?

Her mum goes on. 'And it was so silly of me to forget you don't like prawns. I am sorry.' Yet, Cathy wonders, what else have you forgotten about me? And each day, does Cathy become a little fainter to her mum? Love does that to people like her mum, doesn't it? It turns everyone around them into little more than ghosts. Their eyes can only hold one person.

'I thought, to make up for it, we could go out for a meal tonight, just the family.' But the family is just her mum, Kate and Cathy. 'Will you do that, Cathy?' Her mother's voice is, as always, soft and yet pleasantly throaty. Actually, her mum's got a lovely voice, everyone says that. 'I love the way your mum answers the phone,' says Mark, 'she's so warm, you want to hug her.' And even when she was being strict, she had a gentleness – both her parents did – which Cathy cherished.

'Oh, Mum,' she cries suddenly, 'how could you do this? He's hideous.'

Her mum gives a sudden smile. 'You're so mature and yet, sometimes, you can be so young. Giles, oh, he's all right.' Her voice is light, yet dripping

139

sentiment. 'Now he's asked me to marry him and that makes me very happy, because I love him.' Cathy squirms. She should be the one talking about love and boyfriends, not her mum. 'Give him a chance, Cathy. I know he's made mistakes. He knows it too. But he's never had children of his own and he thinks you don't like him.'

'I don't.'

'But I know, Cathy, that he wants to be a friend to you.'

'For one awful moment I thought you were going to say, a father.'

'That's what's really wrong, isn't it, Cathy? He's not your father. He never can be. In fact, in many ways he's the complete opposite of your father. Your father was a such a gentleman, so sensible, so reliable.'

'You're making him sound boring.'

'No, Cathy. Not at all. Your father was a remarkable man. But he was taken from us, and now there is Giles, so different and yet, with his own special qualities. Oh yes, he has. And he has made me so happy, Cathy.' Cathy gets up and lets the water run noisily over her cup. 'One day, Cathy,' says her mum, 'you will see that . . . well, you will meet someone special.'

'How do you know I haven't already,' mutters Cathy.

Her mother gets up. 'Oh, tell me, have you . . . ?'

'Not in the boyfriend sense you mean,' says Cathy, 'but yes, there is . . . someone.' She still has her back to her mother but then her mum taps her on the shoulder and whispers, 'Come home.'

Cathy turns round. 'I am home.'

Her mum immediately recoils from her. 'Oh, Cathy, this is so unlike you . . .'

Cathy returns to the sink and starts vigorously washing the other plates. 'This is my home now and Mrs Davies said I could stay as long as I liked. So thanks for calling. I've got to get ready for college.' But then, suddenly, she can't bear her mum to go away. 'Mum. Yes, I will come home – when he's gone.'

There's silence for a moment, then her mum says, in a voice that sounds tired and oddly flat, 'Giles is part of our family now, just like you are, Cathy. That's why we both want you home . . .'

We. There's no getting around that word now. It looms over everything, pushing Cathy further and further away from her mother and down this dark corner, until she's trapped there, with no way out. Suddenly, Cathy is quite alone.

The hairdresser stands behind Cathy with a looking glass. Cathy's heart beats furiously. She's done it now, hasn't she? Then she realises the hairdresser is waiting for a comment. 'It's brilliant, Anna,' says Cathy fervently, as Anna's been really helpful and nice, and she certainly doesn't want to hurt her feelings. Yet, actually, all sorts of doubts are crashing in.

She gets up and, as she's following Anna over to the cash till, she can't resist one more look. So, that tough-looking girl with the skinhead haircut is Cathy. Funny, she'd never have recognised her.

She pays Anna and gives her a two pound tip, then Anna asks conversationally, 'What's your mum going to say, then?'

'I think she'll die,' says Cathy with relish. In a few minutes she'll find out, as she's going round to her mum's house to pick up the rest of her things. And her mum kept saying on the phone how she mustn't just take her belongings and run, she could at least stay and have tea with them. Her mum's acting now as if Cathy's just going off for a little holiday and when "things cool down a bit" Cathy will be back.

But Cathy won't. In fact, this will be the last time she ever walks into that house. Is that why she's given herself this startling haircut? She's not sure. Often, before, she'd stood outside the salon, carefully studying the price-list, and imagined herself transformed into . . . well, anything would be an improvement. But she'd never actually walked inside, until today. So yes, perhaps she does want to shock her mum and Giles. What will her mum say? Maybe she'll cry.

She turns to Anna and, in a low confiding voice, asks, 'You don't think this makes me look like a boy, do you?'

'Oh, definitely not,' cries Anna. 'You can take it.'

'Yes,' says Cathy. 'Well, I'm really glad you did it. Oh, have you got my hair?'

It had been Anna's suggestion. Apparently, quite a few customers when they are being "shorn" like to

142

keep a few locks of their hair as a souvenir. Cathy takes the hair from Anna. It's held in a rubber band and looks rather pitiful. She stuffs it into her pocket. Then she catches another glimpse in the mirror of that stranger. WHAT HAS SHE DONE?

7 *Mark Discovers a Secret*

Friday night. The doorbell. Lauren opens her bedroom door and listens. Her mum's voice, then Jason's. He's here. She stands waiting, like an actress awaiting her cue. There it is. 'Lauren, Jason's here.'

'I won't be a minute.' She gives a little shiver. Jason is waiting downstairs, waiting for her. She wants to savour the moment. She wants it still to be exciting. A final peek in the mirror at that oh so tiny, black mini-skirt. She bought it some weeks ago with Cathy and never dared wear it. But tonight, Jason is taking her (and Cathy) to the end-of-term disco at college. He wasn't at all keen, but she persuaded him. This mini-skirt is his reward.

She walks downstairs. Her mum used to take Jason into the lounge for a stilted conversation and the occasional stiff smile, but now they obviously see him as practically one of the family and let him have a cup of tea with them in the kitchen. Just then the kitchen door bursts open and her father is gazing up at her.

'Well, look at my little girl,' he cries. 'Cor!' She rushes down the remaining steps and into one of his great bear-hugs.

'Will you look at this girl,' cries her dad, gesturing towards her mum and Jason, now behind him. He winks at Jason. 'Hot stuff, eh?' He rumbles with laughter. But Jason doesn't return either the laugh or the wink. Instead, his face has gone deathly pale, just like it does when he's about to hit someone. Then he says in his deliberate, low-pitched voice, which always sounds so menacing, 'You can't wear that.'

'Why can't she?' demands her dad.

Jason ignores him. Instead, he just sends his iciest stare to Lauren. 'Why do you have to wear that?'

Lauren catches her breath. 'Because I like it,' she whispers.

'Take it off,' says Jason.

'Take it off?' echoes her dad. 'Why should she? She looks lovely.' Now he's staring hard at Lauren too.

'Take it off,' repeats Jason.

'No,' says Lauren, but in a voice so faint it's hardly even a whisper.

'Then we're not going out,' says Jason, 'we're staying in tonight.' And he starts walking into the lounge.

'Just who does he think he is, ordering you about like that,' says her dad. 'If I were you I'd go to that party with Cathy. That would show . . . Where are you going?'

For Lauren is already walking back upstairs. 'To get changed,' she says, without even turning round. Then she hears her mum say, 'Best to stay out of it, let them sort it out,' and her dad, slamming the door to the kitchen in reply.

Lauren turns round. She and her mum exchange sympathetic looks then she trudges back into her room. She paces backwards and forwards, still shaken by what's happened – and disbelieving. And all because she's wearing a sexy skirt.

Suddenly she's angry. Downstairs she had been too shocked to feel anything. Now she's fuming. She should have stood her ground. She should have said, 'This skirt is me. This is the way I am. If you can't accept it, then get lost.' She would have said that to anyone else.

There's still time. She can march downstairs now and confront him. Or even better, she could put on her really long black coat over her outfit, that would make a point, wouldn't it?

She flops back on the bed. But she'd worn this skirt for him, no one else. She'd wanted to please him. She still wants to please him. Isn't that awful? That's why, in a kind of trance, she takes off the black mini-skirt and puts on her red dress, a favour-ite, but one people have seen her wear before.

The doorbell again. That'll be Cathy, back from her mum's. They must get a key cut for Cathy.

Lauren had meant to do that last week. Then, a polite knock on the door.

'Oh Cathy, don't knock, this is your room too.' It actually irritates Lauren, the way Cathy's creeping about the house, asking before she does anything. Cathy's Lauren's best friend but she's behaving more like a nervous evacuee. Then Cathy thumps down a suitcase.

'More stuff, I'm afraid, to litter up your room . . .' Lauren's gaping at her now, just like her mum did downstairs. 'You hate it, don't you? Go on, you can say it.'

Lauren gets up, and slowly walks around Cathy. 'But, it's so short,' she cries.

'It's not a skinhead,' says Cathy. 'It's a close-crop, though it looks just like a skinhead, I know.'

Lauren touches Cathy's head. 'Oh wow . . . wow . . . you had this done this afternoon?'

'Yeah, bit of an impulse. You can't believe I've done it, can you?'

'It's not that, it's just such a surprise . . . What did your mum say?' asks Lauren.

'Not much actually.' Cathy sounds disappointed. 'She said she couldn't believe it but she supposes she'll get used to it. Giles asked me when was I getting my nose pierced – he's so funny.' Cathy makes a throwing-up noise, then peers into one of the room's many mirrors. 'No, it's not flattering, is it? It makes my nose stand out more, doesn't it? Anna, that's the girl who cut my hair, said, did I want to go away and think about it. But I said, that's my trouble, I think

147

about things too much.' She perches on the edge of her bed. 'Tell me, what do you honestly think of it?'

Lauren sits down beside her. 'It's just a bit drastic.'

'I know, your mum was pretty amazed. She said, "Oh well, don't worry dear, it will grow back, won't it . . . ?"'

'That is true,' says Lauren. 'In a few weeks your hair . . . I mean it's not like having horrendous drum-stick legs.'

'I think I've got those too,' says Cathy.

'No you haven't, and actually, now I'm getting over the initial shock . . .'

'Don't be kind.'

'I'm not. No, you can take that hair-style. It just makes you look tougher.'

'Good,' says Cathy. 'I want to look tougher.'

'Is that why you did it?'

'Yes, well, maybe. I'm not sure really,' she smiles. 'I just thought it's time people started playing by my rules.'

'Well, no one will mess with you now. You're certainly going to get some looks tonight.'

'I know, that's why I thought I'd just drive you both there and then come back . . .'

'Oh no, Cathy, you can't have a tough haircut and then hide away.'

Cathy considers this. 'You're right,' then she adds, 'even though you've bottled out. You said you were wearing your black mini-skirt tonight.'

The shock of Cathy's new haircut had temporarily

wiped out what had happened downstairs. Now all the feelings come rushing back as Lauren tells Cathy about Jason's reaction to her mini-skirt. To her surprise, Cathy says, 'Poor Jason.'

'Poor Jason?'

'Yes, he's scared of losing you and tonight you looked so sexy, he thought, how could he fight off all your admirers.'

'Don't take his side,' says Lauren.

'I'm not.'

'Yes you are – you're always taking his side these days.'

'No, it's just when you're scared, really scared, this red mist starts to form in front of your eyes and you can't see anything properly, so you just lash out . . . He only did it because he cares.'

'Oh, don't give me that,' says Lauren, but her tone is a little softer. 'I've been thinking,' she goes on, 'I don't think you should wear your normal clothes with your new hair-style. No, you should wear black high heels, black shirt, black leggings and black skirt.'

'Not too gothic,' says Cathy.

'No, because we're also going to give you lots of jewellery and a floaty scarf.'

'But I haven't got a floaty scarf or any decent jewellery.'

'No, but I have,' says Lauren, getting up. 'Come on, Cathy.'

Fifteen minutes later Cathy is actually able to look at herself in the mirror without wincing. 'It's your patterned scarf that really sets it off. I look all right, don't I?'

'You look stunning,' says Lauren. 'Just like Sinéad O'Connor.'

'Oh, I don't look as good as her.'

'Yes, you do, because you've both got really feminine faces. Can I touch your hair?'

Cathy laughs. 'If you like.'

Lauren starts stroking Cathy's hair. 'I love doing this, it tickles your hand . . .'

There's a knock at the door and before Lauren can say, 'Come in,' the door opens. Lauren looks up, expecting her dad – that's very much his style – but instead, sees Jason. Cathy immediately stiffens.

'Guess who I am,' she cries.

Jason circles round her. 'Excellent,' he says. 'Really excellent. Honestly.'

Lauren gets up, hands on hips. 'I've changed, happy now?'

Jason doesn't say anything. He doesn't even apologise. He just gives her one of his slow, wide smiles, then says, 'Shall we go then?'

'Are we meeting everyone there?' asks Cathy.

'Well, Adam's not sure if he's going because it's Friday and all, but Mark and Becky will be there, because Mark's going to ask Tania out tonight.'

'Really?' Both Lauren and Cathy look at him expectantly.

'And do you think she'll say "Yes"?' asks Cathy.

'She's got to say "Yes",' says Lauren.

'I reckon she will,' says Jason. 'Trust Uncle Jason.'

Cathy smiles at him but Lauren doesn't join in. Jason really upset her downstairs and yet he thinks he can just flash her one of his grins and act as if it never happened. But she deserves an apology, doesn't she?

Adam stares at the girl in horror. And she seems so normal, too. You'd never guess she'd just taken out a Patrick Swayze video. Adam stares after her in wonderment. But his films are just totally dismal. How could anyone voluntarily watch Patrick Swayze?

As it is Friday night, the video shop is already full; there are a few couples, a group of lads who've already asked him which videos have got loads of blood in them, and a guy who looks as if he's just stepped out of a knitting pattern for cardigans lingering by the (so-called) adult videos.

Sometimes Adam will try and guess which videos people are going to take out. But mostly, he'll just stare into space and day-dream. At school he learnt how to do that for hours at a time. Only, what's unspooling in his head now isn't a dream. It actually happened.

Even though it's over a month since that day and a half in Brighton, not a second of it has faded. Right now, he's remembering the middle of the night when voices outside his room woke him with a start. He jumped up, heart beating madly, not even knowing where he was at first. And then he gazed down and saw Becky lying beside him. Just then, she half-woke up, looked up at him and gave a sleepy little smile before she drifted to sleep again, her arms tightly wrapped around him, while Adam lay there gently stroking her hair and feeling quite dizzy with happiness. He didn't think he'd fall asleep again, especially as the room was stiflingly hot, but he must have done, for the next thing he remembered was this hefty block of sunlight beaming its way through the faded yellow curtains and then he and Becky, talking and cuddling with everything just so relaxed, so easy.

So often, when Adam saw Becky, it was as if there was a meter ticking away beside them, only another ten minutes allowed here, just twenty minutes there. But right then, it was as if nothing else was happening . . . Two guys loom in front of him. Adam takes the video they've chosen; *Good Fellas* with Robert de Niro. He nods approvingly, then puts the tape into another case, takes their money (all tapes £2.50 on Friday nights) and says, 'That's a brilliant film. Good choice.' At least someone in Cartford has got taste.

Now back to . . . what was he thinking about? What else? Brighton. Next, he remembers them having tea and toast for breakfast and getting the gig-gles over the funny looks they got in their costumes. Then they sat on the beach together, only it wasn't so good then, as they could both hear that meter again, for after the beach, the next stop was the rail-

152

way station. It was hard to say which of them was dreading going home more. But when they got back, Becky's mum was really good about it all. She said to Becky, 'I'm just so pleased you rang me on Friday night and told me you'd missed the train. I don't mind if I know.' There was, predictably, more strife from Adam's parents, but not that much more. In fact, they both seemed a little surprised – and relieved – that he'd come home at all. Perhaps they thought he'd run away. Adam isn't sure.

But every Friday since, he's worked at the video shop until nine o'clock. His parents aren't thrilled about this but they accept it. Tonight, he had thought of going on to the party with Becky and Mark. Now that would really upset his parents, Adam partying on a Friday night, so he talked about it with Becky and they decided they could afford to be generous. He won't go to the party, although he's insisting that Becky goes.

It's funny how good he feels about that decision. Perhaps because it is his decision. And he's doing it, not because he's afraid of his parents, but to show he still respects them. All at once, Adam is feeling more in control of his life. He's earning money, getting slightly better grades at college and although he knows his parents still haven't accepted Becky and him, at the moment there's a kind of watchful truce. Best of all, he and Becky are going back to Brighton, probably at the end of May. Only this time, they're going to take rugs and things, so that they can lie on the beach and watch the sunrise.

The shop door opens and in walk Becky and Mark.

'Just thought we'd come in and say hello, before the party,' says Becky. Adam gives her a swift kiss. Ever since Mark had told Becky that he thought couples who kissed in public were"highly inconsiderate," Adam and Becky have been embarrassed to even hold hands. But when he sees Mark going over to the adult videos, Adam slips his arm around Becky's waist. Then he studies her. She still seems . . . well, it's nothing he can put his finger on, but not quite herself.

'Your hair, you haven't put it up with that black ribbon, like you usually do.'

'No, I thought I'd let it hang loose tonight.'

'And you haven't got any of your mad earrings on.'

'No, well, it's only a college party.' She quickly turns away. These days, she and Adam seem able to read each other's thoughts. And she doesn't want Adam . . . not when he's so happy, so proud of himself. She remembers saying to him on the train back from Brighton, 'Last night was a brilliant idea,' and right away, this smile just took over his face. It's never quite left him. So to tell him now, well, that would immediately cast a shadow over something that was perfect – and must always stay perfect.

Besides, she's not absolutely certain. There's still a chance – and how she's clinging to that chance. Soon she'll have to find out, to know for certain. Then there can be no more putting off a decision. But right now, she'll just go on nursing her secret.

It's not so bad in the day, then she can push it down. It's only at night, when she feels herself sinking beneath the weight of it, that she knows she must tell someone.

But then daylight creeps back and she thinks, but who can she tell? Her mum – and admit that she's been lying to her again. Or Adam, always she comes back to Adam. He's looking at her now, questioningly. He suspects something's wrong, doesn't he? She wants to confide in him so much but she can't, especially when there's still a chance . . .

She calls out, 'Just look at Mark, he can't tear himself away.'

Mark looks up and grins. 'I've seen all of these videos anyway,' he says. Then he does a real Jason strut over to them. Whenever Mark's nervous, he always lapses into a Jason impersonation. And all the way here he's been asking Becky what she thinks of Tania and has Tania ever mentioned Mark to her. Now he's talking to Adam about Tania and Adam's gently teasing him – how normal, how everyday it all sounds. Then Becky sees Mark peering at her. 'See, she's not listening, again. Well I'm just so interesting, aren't I?'

'No, I was,' she says. 'What were you saying?'

'I was saying, when I see Tania I'm going to ask her if she's going out with anyone – I know she's not – and then say, "You ought to go out with me," but as a kind of joke, so then if she goes "No way . . ." '

'She won't say that,' says Becky.

'I'd rather she did. I'd rather she came right out

and said, "I think you've got all the sex appeal of a cockroach". I can't bear it when people wrap things up,' he smiled. 'Of course, in the old days, I'd just have sent Adam over.'

Adam grins. 'Did you know, my mate fancies you. Those were the days. Do you remember when we gate-crashed a party at the college?'

'Oh yeah,' cries Mark. 'We stole everyone's drinks.'

Adam shakes his head. 'We just sat there drinking ourselves into the night, getting rid of everything inside us . . . all the bad stuff, anyway. I was so miserable, then.' He's looking across at Becky again now.

Suddenly, she can't bear it. 'Well, we'll leave you to it,' she says.

Adam looks over at the queue of customers. 'Yeah, I suppose I'd better serve someone,' he says. He kisses her again, a much longer kiss this time, before finally, reluctantly, letting her go.

Outside, she breathes hard. She knows she's on the verge of tears. Hold on, she tells herself. And she's so tired all the time, yet at night she never seems able to sleep. Then Mark suddenly stops walking and stands in front of her. Whenever she goes out with Mark she always wears flat shoes, so he's staring right in her face when he says, 'There is something wrong, isn't there?' He sounds so stern she nearly bursts out laughing.

'No, I'm okay, honestly, Markie.'

'I have this wild fantasy that you're upset about me

getting a girlfriend.' But before she can reply, he's already laughing mirthlessly. 'Of course, I know it's not that, but you are really on edge about something, aren't ya?' Then, all at once, his arm is around her and he's saying, 'Tell me,' so gently, that something breaks inside her. Why is it that people being nice to you always makes you want to cry? And the tears rush out, hot and furious.

Then she sees Mark flourishing a handkerchief like a conjuror and for some reason this makes her smile a little. She takes the handkerchief and sniffs hard, anything to steady herself. Should she tell Mark? He is her best friend. And it'd be such a relief to let someone else help her carry this secret. It's just too crushing a weight for her to bear alone. But then telling someone, even Mark, also makes it more real, somehow. She's still wiping her eyes and deciding when Mark blurts out, 'You're not pregnant, are you?'

'Lauren, hi, how are you?' screams a voice. Now who is that, thinks Lauren, Karen Something. Karen Shaw, that's it, in the year above Lauren at school, set fire to her hair in chemistry once.

Karen Shaw pumps Lauren's arm, then says, both shyly and flirtatiously, 'Hi, Jason. I saw you in the *Comet* recently, didn't I? What was it for?'

Jason shrugs his shoulders. 'Some crime or other.'

She giggles. 'No it wasn't, it was for swimming . . . Oh hello, it is Cathy, isn't it?'

'Yes, it's me,' says Cathy.

'But you look so different – better, I mean . . . It's amazing, isn't it? All you need are some Doc Martens.'

'We think she looks brilliant now,' says Lauren quickly. 'You're not at college, are you, Karen?'

'No, no.' Karen laughs loudly at the very idea, even though they are standing in the college refectory.

Some of the tables have been moved out and those that are left have got little vases of plastic flowers on them. But the room is so crowded that no one is actually sitting around the tables. Instead, people are just surging endlessly around. There's an air of restlessness, of waiting for things to start.

Light snacks and soft drinks are being served in here but despite protests from the students, no booze. This, of course, made drinking alcohol all the more exciting and necessary, as everyone smuggled in their own illicit supplies. Now, wherever Lauren looks there are cans and bottles being passed around. A saggy caretaker looks on gloomily. Two windows in the men's loos have already been smashed. The organisers of this 'event' call out from the edges that the DJ is now starting the disco in the hall. But most people seem to prefer being jammed together in here.

'No, we're gate-crashers,' says Karen, turning to the large guy beside her. 'You remember Mike, don't you?' Before anyone can answer, Mike says, 'I remember Jason, football every Saturday morning-down at the old wreck.' Jason laughs and nods. 'So how are you then, Jason?'

'Sound as a pound, my old fruitcake,' says Jason, grinning around with that cheeky smile of his. Lauren watches him rattle off answers to Mike's questions with his usual gleaming confidence. Has he got wheels? Certainly, a beautiful black Alfa Sud. What Jason doesn't say is that he hasn't passed his test (he takes it again next week) and that he is nowhere near finishing "doing up" the Alfa Sud, partly because getting the parts for it is proving much more expensive than he thought.

No, Jason doesn't tell Mike any of this. But then he doesn't exactly volunteer the information to Lauren. She always has to pull facts like that out of him. For instance, if she asked him is he enjoying himself, he'd reply, 'Yeah, sure.' But is he really? Why does she sense he's not really as relaxed as he appears? Is it those tiny beads of sweat on his forehead (although it is mighty hot in here), or the way he's clasping his can so tightly . . . she's not sure. But then, she doubts if Jason is really keen on big parties, anyway.

In fact, now she thinks of it, Jason usually arrives at a party very late, does his royal entrance, followed by what Lauren terms, "a fly-by", parading around as if he's the top person there. And then it's 'must go, people to see, place to go,' and he's disappeared again. Now he's saying something funny, or maybe it's just the way his face is so alive with humour. No wonder Mike and Karen are laughing, they both

159

think he's great. He is great. But they haven't got a clue what he's really like. Yet, who has? Lauren? But then, look at tonight and the way he suddenly turned on her for wearing a short skirt. And it wasn't so much what he said, it was the way he looked at her, his large eyes suddenly such a dark blue, eyes that could shrivel you into tiny pieces.

She needs to talk to him about tonight. She tried to, when Cathy was getting some petrol. 'My skirt, why did you get so mad about that?' she asked. But he immediately blanked up. He always begrudges telling you anything about his feelings. And he just kept saying, 'That's all sorted out now.'

'I suppose we'd better go and circulate,' says Karen. 'Bye, Cathy, bye, Lauren, I'll ring you,' (why do people always say that? Lauren knows she won't) then her voice soars, 'Bye, Jason.' She gives Jason a kiss, then Mike shakes hands with him before they bob out of view.

'Got some fans there, Jason,' says Cathy.

'That girl came into the shop once,' says Jason. 'She's about as subtle as a sledge-hammer.'

'Why, what did she say?' asks Lauren.

'She sort of wiggled up to me, asked something about trainers, then goes, "By the way, are you having an affair with anyone?" ' Lauren half-laughs. She thought that Karen fancied Jason. That's probably why she came over. Jason quickly changes the subject. 'Have you seen Markie yet?'

'No,' says Cathy. 'I thought he'd be here long before now, especially as Tania's been wandering about asking where he is.' Then she adds, 'Is anyone else hungry? I ate hardly anything at my mum's and now I'm starving.'

'Let me get you something,' says Lauren. She's feeling both protective and proud of Cathy tonight. Cathy's never had so much attention, most of it flattering. Yet she senses that Cathy is rather over-whelmed by it all. 'This is my treat and no jokes about moths flying out of my wallet, Jason.'

He looks mock-indignant. 'I haven't said a word.'

'So what do you want Cathy, crisps, peanuts, chocolate?'

'Anything.'

'Jason?'

'Yeah, I'll have a peanut – if you can afford it.'

'Well, we can always share one,' says Lauren. 'I won't be long.'

'Need a hand?' asks Jason.

'No,' says Lauren. She'd rather Jason stayed with Cathy. She figures Cathy needs a bit of support tonight. She's pushing her way over to the refectory when a voice calls out, 'It's the lady in red.' She turns round to see Russell and another boy from her English group, Damian, grinning at her. Russell is wearing a cravat, a green blazer and grey trousers. Damian is sporting an Oxfam suit and an apologetic smile. He always looks vaguely embarrassed, yet he can be quite witty; they're both distinctly clever and regard themselves as "intellectuals". In their own way, they pose about as much as Jason, yet they've

161

also been so helpful to her (and Cathy) Lauren rather likes them.

'So what are you doing here?' asks Lauren.

'Slumming,' replies Russell, promptly.

'And I thought you hated parties like this,' says Lauren.

'We do. We're the guys you always find in the library at parties,' grins Damian. 'But, this young damsel here insisted on dragging us out. You haven't met Emily, my next door neighbour, who's coming to this hall of learning in September, mad fool. Emily, this is the fabulous Lauren.' A girl in a skirt, even shorter than the one Lauren wanted to wear, smiles at her.

'You're not on your own, are you?' asks Russell.

'No, I'm with Cathy,' she says, pointing over.

'But what's happened? She's bald,' Russell cries.

'Being bald is a sign of wisdom, though,' says Damian.

'She's not bald,' cries Lauren. 'She looks lovely. I'm also with Jason,' she adds, pointing again.

'What, the tall guy?' asks Emily. Lauren nods. 'Oh, he's gorgeous, isn't he?'

'Well, yes he is,' says Lauren, proudly.

'I'm afraid Emily is still in her Tom Cruise phase,' says Russell airily.

'I just like good-looking men,' says Emily. 'Have you been in the disco yet, Lauren?'

'No,' says Lauren.

Immediately Russell and Damian stiffen. Lauren notices it but Emily doesn't as she babbles on. 'Well,

162

it's practically empty except for one of your lecturers, who's in there with his arms all around this girl he teaches. If a teacher did that at our school there'd be such a scandal . . .' And even before Lauren asks the name of the lecturer, she knows whose name they are going to say; GRANT. Her first reaction is relief – she nearly walked into that disco. How embarrassing that would have been. But then she glances around and notices Anna and some other girls from her ex-English group staring right at her. She wonders how long they've known about Grant being here with a student – probably ages. She pictures them all gathering round, tearing the legs off that morsel of gossip.

'Who's the girl Grant's with?' she asks.

'Some nonentity,' says Russell. 'Tricia something.'

'Tricia Williams,' says Lauren. That doesn't surprise her. Then, just for a second, she feels a flutter of jealousy. That's followed by a surge of relief, that she's finally away from Grant and his English group. All that is behind her. She must look forward.

She takes a couple of steps towards Russell and Damian and Russell says, 'All evening I've been wondering which lecturers are going to spring up. Can you imagine some of those old maths lecturers here?'

'I can,' says Damian, 'creaking up behind you, asking, "Want to hear a funny story about Pythagoras".' Lauren laughs and can feel herself starting to relax. It was just such a shock hearing that Grant was here. She just won't go anywhere near that disco tonight.

Emily says, 'I think our maths teacher's an alcoholic because we're always finding beer mats in our exercise . . .' but she's interrupted by a girl yelling, 'Look everyone, it's raining,' as she shakes her newly opened bottle about. Lauren ducks away, falling on to Russell. He playfully puts his arms around her but there's an excited look in his eyes too. And Lauren realises, with a glimmer of pleasure, that yes, Cathy's right, he has got a crush on her. Well that's cool, she can handle that.

'I'd better go,' she says.

'Lauren, before you go,' says Russell quickly, 'we're planning a trip up to town to see *A Midsummer Night's Dream* at . . .'

'Regents Park,' prompts Damian.

'We're getting tickets tomorrow, so if you'd like a night of culture and us . . .'

'Well, yes, I might,' says Lauren, with a teasing smile. After *Jules and Jim* which he said he'd enjoyed, Jason had promised to take her to more films and plays in London but he hadn't. So why shouldn't she go with them? 'When are you going, then?'

Russell looks at Damian. 'Well, any day really. What day suits you?' Before Lauren can reply, everyone's attention is seized by a large hand tapping Russell on the shoulder and a most familiar voice saying, 'Can I help you at all, mate?' Jason's smiling but there's a definite air of menace around him too.

Russell looks up and then asks weakly, 'Are you Jason?'

'I claim that honour.' Then Jason says to Lauren, in a low, even voice, 'How about getting that food you promised us. We're starving.'

Lauren feels herself flush with embarrassment. But she's already being pushed away by Jason who she sees is now shaking with anger.

'What the hell are you playing at, pretending to get some food and sneaking off . . .'

'I didn't sneak off. They called me over and I chatted to them, as people do at parties.'

'Don't tell me that guy doesn't fancy you.'

Lauren falters. 'Well, in a little way but it doesn't mean anything.'

'Oh no, with your arms all around him.'

'It wasn't like that.' Then she adds as firmly as she can, 'And you just humiliated me – and yourself. That's why I'm going to calmly go back over there and finish my conversation.'

'No, you're not.'

'Why?'

'Because you've got no reason to talk to them.'

'How can you say that,' cries Lauren. 'They're friends of mine from my English group.'

'So? This is not an English lesson, they've got nothing to say to you here.'

Lauren gazes at him incredulously. He's joking, isn't he? But one more glance at those freezing blue eyes disproves that theory.

'You've no reason to talk to them when I'm here,'

Jason cries and there's just the tiniest crack in his voice when he says it. He reaches out to her again, but this time she pulls away from him.

'No,' Lauren shakes her head. 'No, Jason, you can't do this, saying what skirt I can and can't wear, telling me who I can talk to. I was having a perfectly innocent conversation and I'm going over to finish it and you can't stop me.'

'If you go over there I'm out of that door,' says Jason.

Lauren hesitates, then cries, 'Well go, then. I'll have more fun without you anyway.' Immediately those last words are out she regrets them. But he's already stalked off.

Cathy is watching this scene anxiously. She can't hear what Jason and Lauren are saying, but she can guess. When Lauren fell into Russell's arms, Jason just went charging off. But maybe Cathy can smooth this over, explain to Jason . . . Out of the corner of her eye she watches him push his way to the door. Should she follow him? But first she'd better finish talking to Tania, who's saying. 'I wanted to ask you, Cathy, because you've known Mark for a long time. What's he like?'

'Mark . . . he's just a really nice person, very caring and funny. He's got so many good qualities.'

'That's what I thought you'd say,' Tania goes on. 'Only . . . well, I expect Jason told you that Mark was going to ask me out tonight.'

'He told me something like that,' says Cathy.

'So where is he?'

That's the very question Cathy's asking about Jason. For he's disappeared out of sight now. He's not going home, is he? Not over something so silly.

'I mean, I thought Mark would have been here ages ago,' cries Tania plaintively, 'if he really cared.'

'He will be here,' says Cathy, squeezing Tania's hand. 'Trust me on that point – and I know he cares about you. I'll be back in a minute. I'd just better see where Jason's gone.'

Cathy rushes out of the refectory and down the steps into the reception. There, the queue of people waiting to have their hands stamped is snaking out of the door and towards the car park now. Jason, of course, refused to have his hand stamped. And when the guy said, 'Well, you won't be able to get back in again,' Jason replied, 'I'll get back in if I want to.'

So where has he gone? He's not anywhere here. And neither, to her surprise, are Mark and Becky. Would he have gone into the disco? He's an excellent dancer but he needs a few drinks first. No, he's much more likely to be hanging about outside. But there's no sign of him outside either. Cathy is quickly spotted though.

'Cathy, over here,' calls a voice. It's Louise from her Communications group. She has her arms around a boy Cathy doesn't recognise.

'I just wanted to tell you,' says Louise, 'that I think you look brilliant.'

'Oh thanks, Louise.'

'And that I really admire you for getting your hair

cut like that. I'd just be too scared to do it. I bet you feel completely different, don't you?'

Cathy nods, but actually she's not sure about that. There have been moments tonight when she has felt wilder, more powerful, somehow. Yet, at other times she's felt just like the old Cathy, feeble and anxious. It's as if she can't hold on to herself tonight. She keeps slipping out of focus. She says, 'Goodbye,' to Louise, then walks on to the town centre. She'll just check Jason isn't hanging around there.

It's a dark grey night and the wind is energetically blowing pieces of rubbish into the air. Around her lurks the beginning of Cartford town centre. Only the mortality rate among shops here is so high, it's more like a cemetery. Last week the bakery, which she's visited, well, forever, suddenly expired. She looks again at the small obituary in the window, a typed note stating that "The Bakery has ceased trading". Then she views the remains of the bookshop, recently taken over by "Swag Shop", one of those awful bargain basement places, with their sleeveless vests for £1.99 and their leggings that never reach your ankles, and that crackling disembodied voice shouting out at you about this week's bargains.

No, all the little shops are being choked up, except one. There it stands, so smug, so confident, with its newly painted sign, YOUR FAMILY BUTCHER. She walks quickly on, scanning the town centre for Jason. But he's nowhere to be seen. In fact, there's no one about tonight, not even any boys fighting by the fountain. They must all be at college.

She trudges back. And there it is again. YOUR FAMILY BUTCHER. All that cruelty to animals going on and on. And what's Cathy done to stop it? Handed out a few leaflets, that's all. Cathy gives a sudden cry of frustration, picks up a stone and then sees the stone fly from her hand and hurl itself against the window. She watches in total astonishment. Did she really do that? She must have, for the sound of the glass smashing is still exploding inside her head. She should run away before anyone comes. She can't. She just stands there, seemingly hypnotised by what's happened.

There's a small hole in the window about the size of a tennis ball. But all over the window, tiny cracks are forming; it looks strange, like a spider's web. She rubs her eyes. Perhaps if she rubs them hard enough none of this will have happened. Instead, she lets out a cry. She's just felt a hand on her shoulder.

She whirls round, then laughs with relief. 'You,' she cries. 'I've been looking for you. That window. I can't believe I . . .' she stops. Jason is staring at her while laughing softly in his throat. It's oddly attractive. Now he's running his hand over her hair.

'Why does everyone want touch my hair?' cries Cathy. She feels nervous but also excited or 'juiced up' as Jason would say. Perhaps that's why she suddenly leans forward and kisses Jason gently on the lips. All at once the kiss starts to grow as Cathy feels great waves of tenderness rolling over her.

And afterwards – well, normally kissing makes Cathy gasp slightly, as if she's just been under water.

But now she feels – how can she describe it – just as if she's woken up on a beautiful summer's day. What a strange sensation it is. She's been awakened by a kiss like a character in a fairy tale. Cathy, the sleeping beauty. No, sorry, that doesn't fit. For in all the books Cathy's seen, she doesn't look anything like her. How about Cathy, the sleeping skinhead.

No, Cathy wants to be the sleeping beauty. And just for this moment that's what she feels she is. Then she wonders, when the Sleeping Beauty woke up, did she start trembling like Cathy is doing now and did she feel suddenly, absurdly, unsteady on her feet, as if at any moment she'd keel over with sheer happiness?

She gazes up at Jason, willing him to kiss her again. But he doesn't, he just says, 'We'd better go.' Then, to her surprise, he puts his arms around her. And it feels so natural, so right. That surprises her even more.

They walk away. Cathy hasn't a clue where they are going, she doesn't care. Until a voice explodes, 'STOP! STOP!' Such an ugly sound. Where's it coming from? Then Jason says, 'I don't believe it.' And Cathy turns round to see two policemen steaming towards them.

'Then yesterday, I actually walked into the family planning clinic.' Becky looks at Mark. They are in the hut, lying on a rug. One tiny candle flickers uncertainly beside them. Otherwise, they are in darkness.

170

'So what happened?' asks Mark.

'Well, they had this very smiley person on reception and she asked me to wait in this corridor. So I sat down and all over the walls they had these posters advertising diseases, well, not advertising diseases, you know what I mean. And even under this picture of a couple getting passionate, there were these really depressing facts, which made it just seem so horrible. And I thought, I can't stay here.' She pauses.

'So you walked out,' says Mark.

'Actually, I ran out.' There's another silence. 'After all, I might not even be pregnant, might I? Just because I missed my period . . . it could be stress . . . or anything.' The brightness in her voice fades. 'But if I am pregnant, can you just imagine all the gossip.' She rubs her hands over her face. 'And I'll have to tell my mum.'

'Your mum's all right,' says Mark.

'Yes, she'll be okay about it, in the end, but still, it's just so awful having to tell her something like that.'

'Will you tell your dad?'

'I don't care about him. He'll just say, "Oh, Becky, what are you doing, giving me this stress." Then he'll see Adam, no, he'll ring Adam, and give him a right ear-bashing, because, according to him, it'll be Adam's fault.' She makes a tiny fist and hits it against her chest. 'Oh, Mark, what a mess.'

Mark gets up. The candlelight reminds him of when, years and years ago now, they all sat round telling ghost stories. He suspects he is better at telling ghost stories then he is at giving advice. For he's hardly said anything to Becky. But what can he say? He's still a bit stunned by it all. When he asked her if she was pregnant, it was just a wild guess, really. He knew something was wrong but . . . Adam a father? That's a shock. Somehow, Mark hadn't thought of any of them having children until they were at least thirty. He starts to pace up and down. If it helps Jason, he thinks it might help him now. He peers around the hut. He can make out Adam's old cassette player and tapes, a pile of books he doesn't recognise. This hut really belongs to Adam and Becky now, doesn't it? He's just a guest here.

'I know Adam and I should have been more careful,' says Becky suddenly.

'You didn't practise safe sex?' says Mark, mock-solemnly, waving a finger at her. But Becky isn't smiling and Mark wishes he hadn't said that.

'I don't regret what's happened, Mark, not a second of it. I just wish . . . It's so unfair, isn't it?' Mark doesn't answer. On the train home from Brighton he could hardly talk to Cathy, he was so sick with jealousy. And at home, he was really nasty. His mum kept saying, 'I don't know what's got in to him.' Then he tried to go to sleep. But he couldn't lie still. His head was pounding too much.

The first time Becky had gone out with Adam, it was as if she'd started going up a ladder, leaving Mark behind. But not too far behind. He could still climb up and bring her back – until that night in

Brighton. All at once she was so far from him, she was out of sight. He could spend a lifetime climbing that ladder and still never reach her now.

So he paced about his bedroom in the darkness, plotting how he'd behave the next time he saw Becky. He was going to be so cool and distant. He would freeze her out. That'd teach her to abandon him and go off with her boyfriend for a night of torrid passion.

But then, on Monday he saw her in the town centre and she rushed over to him with such a glow about her that, right away, he was melting faster than a snowball in a microwave. Pathetic, really. And now, he's the only one to know her secret and so far, he hasn't said one worthwhile thing. He decides to try now.

'Becky, you've got to sort this out, you know, get it out of the way. I mean, you're wasting time now.' He hesitates, then plunges on. 'There was a girl at my old school who thought she was pregnant but didn't check it out. She didn't tell anyone and no one suspected for ages, but she's paying for it now.'

Becky sits up. 'How do you mean?'

'Well, for a start, all her teeth fell out because she didn't get any supplements . . .' he stops. Becky is laughing. 'Don't laugh at me,' he says, indignantly.

'I'm sorry, Mark,' says Becky. 'It's just, it's so horrible.' Becky taps her teeth. 'They're still all right, so far,' she says. They're both laughing now and Mark falls down beside her again.

'You look yourself again, now,' he says.

'Do I? You know me pretty well, don't you?' says Becky. 'How long have we been here?' She holds her watch up to her face, then exclaims. 'It's ten o'clock. But the party! You're supposed to be asking Tania out.'

'Can't be helped,' says Mark lightly.

'Mark, this is all my fault. I've ruined it for you.'

'No, no,' he grins. 'I'll just tell her you carried me off to have your wicked way with me.'

'But I feel awful about this.'

'Forget it, she'd probably have turned me down anyway.' Then he clears his throat and says, 'Becky, I'll go with you, if you like, to the clinic.'

She stares at him. 'Mark, would you really . . . it'd be so much better if I had someone . . . if I had you there with me.'

'I can blindfold you in the waiting room, can't I?' He sits forward eagerly, 'and I'll book the appointment for you, if you like.'

'No, no, that's okay. I'll do that.'

'Tomorrow,' he says.

'Yes, Mark, tomorrow.'

'No, Jason, I can't let you do this,' whispers Cathy. He doesn't answer, just hugs her tighter.

'I've got to say something,' she cries, in a kind of whispered shout.

'No, Cathy,' he says firmly. He relaxes his hold on her. 'Trust me. It's all under control.' She hears the policemen calling him and shivers. But he is grinning all over his face. Then he reaches into his

174

pocket and pulls out his dark glasses. Now she's smiling and shaking her head. Only Jason can wear sunglasses at eleven o'clock at night and somehow carry it off. He turns to the small crowd who are standing outside McDonald's watching and gives them a quick wave, then saunters over to the police car, still grinning.

He's really high, thinks Cathy. But still, it's she who should be sitting in that police car now, not Jason. Yet, the policemen knew Jason from sabbing and just assumed it was he who'd smashed the butcher's window. They weren't very interested in Cathy and when Jason said she'd had nothing to do with it, they seemed to accept that. She suspects they want to interrogate Jason to try and get the names and addresses of other hunt saboteurs. So why didn't she speak up? Why couldn't she locate her voice. Why?

'Cathy,' Jason calls out of the car window. Cathy rushes forward. 'Tell Lauren I'll ring her tomorrow, will you?' Lauren. That's a shock. But why? She's his girlfriend and of course, her best friend, who is very kindly putting her up. And how does Cathy repay Lauren's kindness, only by snogging with her boyfriend. But Cathy's always kissing and hugging Adam and Mark, they're close friends. Just like Jason is . . . there it is again, that jolt of excitement she gets, just by saying his name. This is so awful, isn't it? And it's all Cathy's fault. Just what was she doing, kissing him like that? But Jason – well he helped, didn't he? What did that kiss mean to him? Nothing. He'll have forgotten it already – won't he?

Now the police car is driving away. There's a cheer from the crowd outside McDonald's. And then Cathy starts cheering too. All right, Jason likes rescuing people but still, he's doing this for her. She cheers again and follows the car, waving madly, while he's just sitting back, smiling away.

Now he's gone. The crowd move away. Cathy starts wondering if he's smiling now. Will they really interrogate him for the names of the other sabs? How could she let him do this?

She turns round, to see Lauren walking towards her.

Don't miss *Friends Forever IV: Everything Changes*.

In this, the most dramatic book of the series, all the characters find their lives changing.

Will Jason and Lauren stay together?

Which ambition comes true for Mark?

Why do Adam and Becky find their lives turned upside down?

And will Jez return?

Pete Johnson

I'D RATHER BE FAMOUS

I don't want to just fade away down some back street, with Adam, and then end up on a gravestone with no one remembering who I am. I want to make my mark, show everyone I'm here and sign at least a few autographs before I die.

Jade is sixteen-and-a-half, with a steady boyfriend called Adam and a sometime job selling videos. But it isn't enough. Jade's problem is that she has very little talent, but she knows she can be a TV presenter. All she needs is one lucky break. Then Jade hears a dating show is looking for applicants. Adam would go crazy if she ever applied. So dare she? Jade dares . . . and her life will never be quite the same again.

Pete Johnson

ONE STEP BEYOND

Sometimes you're walking right on the edge and don't even realise it.

Like Alex. He's waited five years to take revenge on Mr Stones.

And Natasha. She's always done what her parents tell her – until the day she turns sixteen.

Then there's Yorga. He has a brilliant idea to stop the hated Casuals taking over his town.

Just three of the people who don't realise they're right or the edge – until they take one step beyond.

A collection of eight dazzling stories of love, revenge, laughter and horror.

Pete Johnson

THE COOL BOFFIN

A boffin, of course, is an incurable swot . . . He swots and swots while the world passes by in a blur . . . That was me . . . And then, one day something happened – something weird and scary.

Richard Hodgson thinks he is instantly forgettable. His schoolmates don't even seem to know his name – they just call him 'Boffin'. How he longs to change his boffin image.

Then a dramatic accident gives him his chance. The Boffin becomes 'Ricky' – cool, sharp and a bit of a lad. He enters an alien world of wild parties and girls. But things are not always what they seem . . .

"A deftly written and well-paced story . . . the dialogue is sharp and witty. One to be read and talked about."

British Book News

"There is genuine character development here."
Times Educational Supplement

"Devastatingly funny."
Books